# <u>Simple but Effective: A Guide</u><br><u>your Child's Behav</u>

*A concise yet comprehensive manual for the behaviour management of children of all ages.*

**By Peter Allerton**

**www.peterallertonwriter.blogspot.co.uk**

This book is dedicated to every hardworking parent on the planet. You are deeply appreciated (even if nobody shows it!).

First Published by Peter Allerton Publishing 2021

# Contents

**Children's Stories by Peter Allerton**

# 1 - INTRODUCTION

Dear Parents and Caregivers,

Welcome to this 'manual' of **hints, tips and strategies** on how to help your children with their behaviour and learning at home. Over 20 years in the making, I've been looking for ideas throughout my teaching career, 'cherry picking' the most practical and effective ones for this book (in which I try to avoid any jargon or dense theory). Every suggestion in this book is **tried and tested**. This aims to be a practical guide, not an academic thesis.

I sincerely hope you will find at least something useful to assist you in probably the most important and challenging (and definitely worst paid) job in the world!

Managing your child's behaviour can feel like a complicated process but this guide aims to make it as **simple and straightforward** as possible by outlining the key principles and suggesting practical methods that should help (the challenge will be actually sticking to them).

There is **no such thing as a perfect** parent or child. We are all human and each have our own strengths and weaknesses, it is what makes us unique and keeps life interesting. You cannot know everything and cannot get it right all the time. This book is just a guide to help give you an edge and make things a little bit easier whenever possible.

I am delighted that you have chosen to read this book as there is nothing I want more than to help parents raise their children with less stress and worry in the long run, the ideal outcome of which being that these kids may have **a more positive impact** on the world around them.

I have always found the **general lack of support**, training and help for parents to be quite ludicrous, especially given the significant impact of the 'job'. Rather, most onlookers can be very quick to judge others who are often just doing their best in difficult circumstances with little or no guidance. Personally, I feel basic parenting skills should at least be a part of the core curriculum at high schools everywhere.

Having worked closely with thousands of students and their parents over the years, I am hopeful there should be **something for everyone** somewhere in this guide. Improved behaviour **also helps improve your child's learning**. This becomes an upward cycle where the child gains esteem through being more self-disciplined and positive, which in turn can lead to being more successful at school as they gradually develop their critical thinking skills, patience, attention, etc.

There will be some trial and error involved and obviously not all ideas will work well for everybody, but if you find even just one strategy to make a positive difference, then I hope the relatively small amount you have invested in both time and money to read this guide **will have been worth it**.

Give each option **a real try**. Don't just think 'Oh well we tried it once, but it didn't work.' All new strategies can take time and effort to become effective but once they are, they should invariably save you far more stress and hassle **in the long term**.

The principles and ideas that run throughout this book apply to the fundamental parent-child relationship, so **can be used at almost any age**. Positive parenting strategies can **work well with every child** regardless of their background or temperament.

This guide can be read from cover to cover or you can just try to pick bits out if you don't have the time. However, I do recommend trying to **at least skim through the whole thing** at some stage as most sections are relevant to each other. There is quite a bit of **'overlap' between the various topics**, as many of the ideas are naturally interlinked.

Finally, thank you for reaching out. Some parents are too proud or embarrassed **to seek any sort of help** or guidance. I know you are often under a lot of pressure in a largely thankless task so that is perfectly understandable, but it never hurts to try a new approach or look for new ideas, especially as the outcome could be immensely beneficial in the end.

(Disclaimer: any advice offered in this book is advice only. It is up to the reader how it is implemented and the author bears no responsibility for any particular outcome).

# 2 - REASONS BEHIND BEHAVIOUR

**All kinds of behaviours occur for a reason.** Often, children display challenging behaviour as a way to meet their needs. It is important to try to understand WHY the behaviour might be happening in order to deal with it appropriately.

Understanding why a particular type of behaviour might be happening can **help you choose which strategies to use** and which alternative choices you can offer your child. Without being able to identify the problem behind the behaviour, it can be more difficult to identify a suitable solution.

Behaviour **may occur for one of these** four common reasons: Escape, Attention, Tangible Items, and Reinforcement.

ESCAPE – challenging behaviour is **used by the child to escape** from situations, tasks, or even people. For instance, if they want to get out of doing something, i.e. maths homework or going to bed.

ATTENTION – i.e. **to get attention** from a parent, teacher or peer. Attention comes in different forms, for instance if they feel you are giving more attention to their sibling they may 'act up' to get more from you. **Negative attention is still attention**.

TANGIBLE ITEMS – to **gain access to** a wanted tangible item (i.e. a toy, iPad, candy, etc.).

REINFORCEMENT – the behaviour is **internally reinforcing** to the child (it helps them to release stress, even though it might lead to more problems afterwards).

Behaviour is **a form of communication**. It is important to observe and try to understand your child's behaviour. A certain type of behaviour might appear the same but can have different reasons behind it, or vice versa.

Often challenging behaviour can come **from feelings of insecurity or frustration** (even if they appear very cocky, this can be an overcompensation to mask fear or insecurity), and the behaviour itself cannot be properly resolved without getting to the real cause behind it. Children (and indeed adults) may **compensate for any feelings of inadequacy** with disruptive, abrupt or shy and withdrawn behaviour.

The best way to resolve such issues is **through talking**, but only when you are both calm and feel you can listen to each other. This can take time. **Ask them what's bothering them** to find what might be behind the behaviour as well as help them be able to talk through it.

Try to focus on the child '**underneath the behaviour.**'

# 3 - PRINCIPLES OF BEHAVIOUR MANAGEMENT

*This section is **a combination of key ideas** that apply to more than one area of the book. Also, many points made throughout this guide can apply to more than one section so it is advisable to try and at least skim through all of the sections when you can find the time.*

**NEVER negotiate**. This is crucial. For instance, if they argue with you, deal with the rudeness first. Once you re-establish your authority (as they acknowledge the implied hierarchy of the parent-child relationship), you can resume giving the instruction or resolving the situation at hand – but only after the issue of the rudeness has been resolved.

Behaviour can often **be about power**. If you do argue with them, this drags you down to their level. Never accept disrespect. If you argue back, you are thereby accepting their rudeness and thereby diluting your authority.

Even if you do end up arguing with them, you can rarely win as they are less restrained by logic, and for them it can often be **all about winning** and gaining some power rather than being factually correct, which will only add to your sense of frustration. For instance, they can keep screaming all day how the sky is pink with yellow dots even if they themselves can see it's blue, just in order to wear you down until they've 'won'.

**Always try to appear calm and positive** – if they see you are upset, they know they are getting to you. Managing to do this also models desired behaviour.

If you become angry, take a step back. **Do not act in anger**. Remember, their behaviour is THEIR problem, not yours (if possible you can also 'tag a partner in' until you calm down).

Make it clear **it is their behaviour you are disappointed with, not them**. They are letting themselves down, not you.

**Be their parent not their friend**. They **feel safer with boundaries** and once established can enjoy doing positive things independently within them.

Be positive and proactive in your instructions and expectations – **pre-empt rather than react**.

Make them **WANT to have** good behaviour.

Be **'firm but fair'** – some kids can unfortunately see kindness as a weakness and instinctively attempt to exploit it. If you remember from your time at school, often the 'firm but fair' teacher was the one students eventually respected most.

Even though your child should know you love them unconditionally, kindness from you should only **happen when they are also being nice**, or at least not being difficult. Give them every opportunity to be nice so you can enjoy being nice in return.

Behaviour is a form of communication. Especially with younger children, by talking and modelling positive behaviour you can help give them with the words and actions they need **to better express themselves**.

If you do what you can to assist them in feeling **more relaxed and safe**, there should be less disruption.

Parenting can be a question of **finding a balance** between caring for your child while also granting them autonomy whenever possible.

Different approaches **may work for different** children in a family.

The **rules many need to change** as they grow up.

Avoid confrontations and **power struggles** – try not to get involved in any attempts at mind games.

Have you heard of '**Grandma's rule**' before? It's a very simple but effective way to describe a positive reward system, i.e. 'If you eat your vegetables, you can have dessert.' Applying this rule insistently and consistently is the challenge.

Teach them to **treat others how they want to be treated** themselves.

# 4 - BOUNDARIES

Often bad behaviour can be a case of them **testing boundaries** or trying to gain power / be in control **rather than anything malicious**, especially in little ones.

Deep down **kids need boundaries**. They **feel safer with them**. need to know where they are and what's supposed to be happening. That's one reason they're always pushing against them. They like to know how far they can go so they need to know what the limit is.

Once they know the boundaries, you **can have more fun together** within those boundaries. **This also helps establish rapport.** However, as soon as they step outside, you need to **remind them immediately**.

Children **can feel chaotic and unsettled** if boundaries are inconsistent or not evenly enforced, or clearly marked.

Have clear boundaries that are **fair and age appropriate**.

Try to express your expectations in a way that shows **you will back up what you say**.

You **can say no kindly**. It is good to set boundaries and you are in fact doing them a favour with this, especially in the long term. Remember **it is their choice** how they react. **Stand your ground**, for their benefit as well as your own.

It may **take some time** for them to adjust to the new boundaries and expectations (set them gradually).

# 5 - INSISTENT AND CONSISTENT

**Be INSISTENT and CONSISTENT**. This is vital and even if initially rather grinding, will make life much easier as things progress.

Be consistent – always maintain the same expectations, **don't sometimes let things go** because you're tired or can't face an unpleasant interaction, as once they learn they can bend the rules, you will be even more tired and face more unpleasant interactions in the future for sure. You simply MUST remain insistent and consistent at all times, otherwise you will be making things far **more difficult for yourself later on**.

It is a simple choice of **sticking with the strategy** and being tired now but less tired later, or not sticking with the strategy and being tired now and exhausted later!

**Beware** your bad or tired mood affecting your consistency.

Of course, at times being too 'pushy' can be **counter-productive**. My own parents were obsessively strict about punctuality, to the point where I have been late for almost every appointment since leaving their influence!

# 6 - IT'S THEIR CHOICE

Many children after 'acting up' will blame their negative behaviour on external factors **rather than take personal responsibility for it.** This is a crucial aspect to overcome. Many criminals in court will blame just about anyone and everything before they might admit guilt, and while hopefully your child will never be in such a situation, it is vital to 'nip' this trait in the 'bud' early on.

It is extremely important to stress that **their behaviour is THEIR choice**. Lead them to see the situation this way.

**Give them a choice**. Their behaviour then becomes their responsibility. Then their behaviour is up to them, not you.

Make the choice **clear to them**.

The choice must be **simple, realistic and non-negotiable**. i.e. 'You can keep crying and stay in the car, or take a few deep breaths, say sorry to your sister and we can go into the shop together.'

If they **know the consequences** when they make the choice, they must accept them afterwards.

Encourage them to **STOP. THINK. DO.** i.e. Stop acting up, think about what they are doing, make their choice. You can label what they decide to do as Good choices and Poor choices, and reward / punish them accordingly.

**Empathise:** i.e. 'I know you don't want to, but we really need you to make a good choice and put your shoes on. Then your feet won't be hurt.'

Try to **avoid giving ultimatums.** They must be choices. Not 'If you don't stop running around I'm going to take your toys away!' but rather 'Please sit down instead so you can continue playing.'

Give a CHOICE before a WARNING, **give a WARNING before** a CONSEQUENCE. Why? Because then the child is **solely responsible for their actions** and cannot blame the consequence on anyone else. Some children need time to process and respond to the choice, hence the warning before the consequence.

You can **ask them why** they think they're about to be told off, so they can already start to reflect and take responsibility. This can also save you having to explain something to them that **they should already know**.

Seek to ensure your child **learns to equate** poor choices with feeling bad and good choices with feeling good. Kids want to do whatever they want to do and become upset if they're not allowed. Hence needing such negative and positive reinforcement to help them **regulate their attitude**.

Always do your best to **appear objective**. This tells your child that you are simply disappointed in their behaviour rather than you taking it personally and making assumptions.

Let them know how and why you have **their best interests at heart** and, while you can understand why they may be acting in a disappointing way, they are **still able** to make better choices and that is ultimately what you are hoping for.

# 7 - CONSEQUENCES

If your child chooses not to follow a rule, then **there must be a consequence**.

**Consequences should be** *fair, consistent, certain, known in advance, logical* and *related to the action.*

Negative behaviour must be **followed by a negative consequence** – just as positive behaviour is followed by something positive. In fact, **positive reinforcement can be more effective**. Have your child 'aiming high' rather than 'looking down'.

Therefore, try to **focus on there being the possibility of positive consequences** more than negative consequences, using **small incentives / increments**. The carrot is often more effective than the stick!

What sort of rewards and sanctions do you have in place for your child now? Are they **agreed upon, reasonable and consistent**? Make sure you and your child are agreed on these, that they have had input in the decision making process, and that they are clear what they are. This can evolve over time while the rewards and sanctions are updated along the way.

**A child's 'want' of things can be as powerful as their 'fear' of things**. Not getting a treat can be **as effective as receiving a punishment**, but has less negative impact and is easier to follow through with.

If children are fearful, this can act out in negative ways. **It can be subconscious**. Threat of punishment can **become a self-fulfilling prophecy**. It is much better if they are aspiring towards a reward or praise instead.

For instance, using the 'colour climbing ladder' (this is explained in Section 18), having kids **aspiring to move up** to blue rather than being afraid of moving down to yellow makes the general atmosphere and their individual mind-set much more positive. Meanwhile the more positive consequences they achieve, **the better their attitude** and therefore behaviour (and subsequently learning) becomes.

**Follow through with everything you say, every time.** If you don't follow through even once, **it undermines** *everything* and makes it harder the next time. If they cry for ten minutes and then get what they want, next time they might cry for twenty minutes because they know there's at least a small chance of it working. On the other hand, if you leave them to it and they give up after twenty minutes, then the next time they're more likely to give up after ten because they know it probably won't work, and so on. So, this works in parallel opposite directions. Essentially, **if you let them 'win', it will be a much bigger struggle next time.**

So, **let them 'cry themselves out' if necessary** (at least metaphorically speaking – obviously this doesn't have to involve actual crying). This can be hugely challenging as a parent but after you've done it once it becomes easier until they eventually give up. Just don't let them see any weakness in your eyes or voice (in case they think that you'll crumble or you're suffering more than them) or **they will continue in the hope** that you might 'crack' first. You can talk with them about what happened after they have calmed down.

When your child is crying, try not to treat it like a fire you need to put out asap. **Crying can be necessary** and self-soothing after an incident, unless they are doing it for effect in which case you need to be careful how you react.

**Feedback not failure** – discuss where they went wrong, rather than just tell them off.

If words fail them when they are trying to explain themselves, perhaps ask them to write a letter to explain or even draw a picture – this **helps them to reflect** on things more, too.

**Avoid delayed consequences**. Remember to **reward or discipline immediately** once they have made their choice. **Avoid delayed consequences**. The younger the child, the more immediate it should be.

A consequence shouldn't feel like punishment **just for the sake of it**.

**Be proportionate and gradual**. Don't bottle things up, let things go for a bit then finally snap and impose a huge sudden sanction. Give the child a chance to make a good choice and recover their behaviour.

Give the child **a chance to make a good choice** and recover first.

**Avoid 'good negative consequences'**. For instance, if a child cries to get attention or be disruptive and you hug them, or refuses to put on their shoes and you end up doing it for them, they will do it more next time because they know it will eventually get a desired outcome. It simply reinforces the challenging behaviour.

You must be **consistent with consequences** such as timeouts or 'groundings' so the child can make the maximum connection between negative behaviour and the sanction – and not just 'sometimes' where it's inconsistent and they know sometimes they'll get away with it or possibly even be punished unfairly on occasion.

Rewards and sanctions need to be made very clear from the start and **reinforced** on a daily basis.

**Keep an eye out** for your child becoming bored with one type of reward or relatively 'numb' to a sanction. Persevere but don't 'flog a dead horse' either. **Tweak things as you go along** rather than give up.

**Always follow up on a warning**, even if it feels unpleasant and might momentarily spoil or disrupt the day.

Avoid changing the rules / punishments **without notice**.

Quite often **the idea of being punished** is enough, rather than the punishment itself. They don't want that negative feeling of being caught or told off.

For younger kids, using a **'time-out' area** as a punishment can be effective. Alternatively, if this doesn't prove effective (occasionally it can be counter productive if they are even more upset and difficult after time outs – though please persevere with it first), you could try a time-in. This is where the child still has to sit in silence but remain near you so they don't feel they are being rejected as well as punished, thereby reducing any further resentment.

It **shouldn't feel like** they are being punished just for the sake of it or out of spite.

Provide **immediate feedback** as to why they're being rewarded or punished to help reinforce the boundaries and remind them it was their choice but they can still make a good choice next time instead.

**Keep any promises you make**, so it is sometimes appropriate to think twice before you make them!

**If they refuse the sanction, increase it.** Be sure to do this **in small increments.** It's just as effective but also leaves *both* of you some 'wriggle room'.

In time **they will learn to associate positive behaviour with being happy, and negative behaviour with being unhappy.** Keep it simple. Negative consequences versus positive rewards. It's simple and obvious which they will prefer.

Initially they might be trying to look like they're rebelling against being punished, at least on the surface as initially they might be craving power rather than approval. But once they realise they can only gain any **power through gaining your approval**, they should gradually start **aspiring to the rewards** rather than battling against sanctions.

It is vital that you allow your child to have to **face the consequences of their actions**. If you continually try to protect them from this, their issues will continue and in all likelihood worsen over time and into adulthood. It is a part of **developing resilience**, something they will need when you are not around to protect them from the ups and downs of life. Try not to wrap them in cotton wool. They need to **develop common sense**. They also need to feel bad sometimes in order to **learn how to make themselves feel better / self-soothe**. It's natural to feel sad or bad. Also, avoid coddling little ones too much. So **do not be afraid** to give out sanctions whenever they are due.

You are **not being mean** by giving out sanctions – **it is for them**, not you. It can be the least conscientious parents who let their kids run wild and do whatever they like, using wanting them to be 'happy' as an excuse. They are not invested enough in the sometimes exhausting emotional struggle to maintain effective behaviour management and raise genuinely happy, well-balanced children.

Don't let them choose **what to do after being difficult**.

**Sanctions for younger children** can include a timeout mat or corner, naughty step, 'go to your room' (this gives you both a chance to calm down), missing a fun activity, moving down a colour or not getting a star on their behaviour chart, not getting to choose what to do next (missing out on something good can be even more powerful than receiving a sanction).

For timeouts, there should be absolutely **no verbal interaction** with the child until near the end of the timeout. Then, ask for **good choice behaviour** and elicit an appropriate response before 'releasing' them.

If a timeout has been given for not following an instruction, the child must **still follow this instruction after the timeout is over**. Otherwise they may equate a timeout to being a trade off with avoiding having to follow the initial instruction.

Give them a **positive option after a sanction**, i.e. if they were snatching, tell them 'Now you can go and ask Harry if you can share the toy.'

Make sure you **ALWAYS follow up on EVERY** warning.

If you make them miss out on doing something, sometimes it can be useful to **give them something constructive** to do instead rather than just let them 'sit and stew'. For instance, they could write a letter explaining why they shouldn't have done what they did and what they're going to do next time instead. Or they could help with household chores, etc.

Be careful **not to use homework** or anything academic as a punishment as it **sends the wrong signal**.

Remember you're **punishing the action, not the child**, make that clear to them, i.e. 'You're grounded because you stole your sister's pocket money' rather than 'You're grounded because you're a selfish thief.'

**Choose the rewards together**.

Often, not receiving a reward **can be punishment enough**.

Keep rewards **small and frequent**.

Rewards must be consistent and **proportionate**.

Rewards should not be for simply not being difficult for a moment, but rather **for doing something that is challenging for them** (so if a child finds it genuinely difficult to settle down to breakfast in the morning, as soon as they finally sit still and start to eat, they have earned their reward).

**Progress the reward system**. i.e. five stickers / stars in one day or week might result in a big reward, like being able to watch a movie of their choice. This can happen the next day if necessary. Indeed, following on the praise the next day also helps remind them of the **positive reinforcement from the day before**. But try not to raise negative behaviour from the day before if you can avoid it. Try to make sure your child **starts each day with a 'clean slate'** (i.e. when using the colour climbing ladder, every day would begin on the neutral middle colour).

Don't worry about **feeling like you have to bribe** your kids to do something in exchange for a reward. If none of us were paid to go into work each day, how many of us would still do it? It can be both realistic and necessary to do so at times.

Choose **a reward that's constructive**, so avoid extra iPad time etc. Try stuff like pancakes in the mall, a trip to the cinema (let them arrange the movie, time, get the tickets, choose the snack, etc.), a choice of sports activities or clubs join (this would help them develop their social and motor skills, give them a hobby and possibly a team to identify by, and gain valuable life experience along the way), an event or place to go to (ideally with others), etc. Maybe while there try having a phone amnesty.

Update or change rewards **if the existing ones gradually become**

**less effective** in motivating behavioural change.

One reward can be **'free choice'**, for example they choose an activity or a treat from an agreed list. On the other hand, there could be a free choice slot in the home routine every day, that could be taken away in the event of any challenging behaviour.

**However, don't take away a reward they received earlier**. For instance, if the child received a reward for good behaviour or effort, but later they do something bad, do not punish the later negative behaviour by taking away the reward for the earlier positive behaviour. Simply give them a separate sanction.

# 8 - COMMUNICATION

**Be a good listener.**

**Make and maintain eye contact**: If they're not looking, they're not really 'listening' or recognising your authority. Get their **attention before speaking**. Make sure they are looking at you. Even if they can hear you, if they're not looking then **they're not acknowledging** you. However, keep in mind sometimes they might be looking away out of deference or embarrassment.

Make sure you **always get** a verbal or at least physical response.

Keep in mind, younger children are **still learning how to communicate** and their language abilities aren't very sophisticated yet. They might act aggressively **in the absence of developed language to communicate** feelings like frustration, anger, confusion or embarrassment.

Encourage your child to **join in adult conversations** if and when appropriate.

Let them know you are **always willing to listen**.

**Validate what they say** (even if you disagree with their opinion, show them respect). This can be a tricky area as sometimes you might feel they are talking nonsense or exaggerating. You don't have to say 'Oh yes, I agree with you entirely', rather just let them know that you are listening. After a while they may well stop resorting to exaggeration as they will feel they can open up to you, **have your attention already** and that you respect what they are saying.

**Ask for their opinion on things**, for instance what you're watching together on TV, something that's happened, a person they've met, a news story, etc.

**Model your thinking**. Demonstrate your thought process, like the contestants tend to do on the TV show 'Who wants to be a millionaire?' For instance, 'Well I could... I wonder if I should... However, what about... Maybe we need to... But then again...' etc.

Let them **practise explaining ideas** or demonstrating their knowledge in their own words.

**Ask them about their day** after school, ask **open questions** and encourage them to expand on their answers. Sometimes they may hide anything unhappy there then take it out on the family once home. If they're feeling down at school, they might **seek to reassert** themselves on their siblings or even parents to regain some sense of control. It will **help if they can open** up about any issues they might be having. Also, many children typically offer the standard response of 'Nothing' when asked what they did that day, so again, ask them to expand on their answers.

**Avoid complaining**. Make it clear that it is their actions you are disappointed with, not them. **They are letting themselves down, not you**.

**Elicit a response from them as much as possible**. For example, every story should involve a question about each page, every new instruction should be checked for understanding. Ask them to explain before transitioning to something new, i.e. if going to play outside, ask them where they are going and what they will do there.

**In the morning** ask them how they are feeling and what they are going to do that day. This sounds simple but it's surprising how seldom kids are asked this. You can follow up by asking if there's anything they're looking forward to or dreading.

**At the end of the day** you can reflect together on anything positive that happened, any concerns they may have, anything they are looking forward to the next day. You can also say if you noticed any positive changes in their behaviour and think about what might have helped make that change.

**Initiate small talk** by asking 'Penny for them?' (as in 'What are you thinking now?'), 'Give us a smile', 'Know any jokes?' and so on.

**Eating together**. Try to eat at the same time and if it has to be in front of the TV, then at least actually talk about what's on, and let them choose what to watch sometimes.

You can **allow a tantrum to play itself out**. Let them get it out without becoming involved in or fighting it, as that can often just escalate things further. Once they've stopped, **then you can talk**. It also shows them the tantrum isn't working. It is also important **so show some empathy** towards them in this moment, as this can actually help them calm down rather than continue to rage against you or whatever it is that's upsetting them.

Try to have many **daily interactions with your child**, no matter how small. They will get a lot more development from taking turns communicating with an adult than they will from a mobile phone screen for instance. Incidentally, try to also be aware of just how much you are on your phone yourself when around your children.

Explain more **clearly how their behaviour affects** you. For instance, rather than yelling 'Shut up!', take a breath and say 'I'm becoming upset because there's too much noise and I'm on the phone'.

## - <u>8.1 - Social Communication</u>

You can talk about and **model expected appropriate behaviour** in different social situations.

Try **discussing possible situations** based on different social and communication scenarios. Ask them what would / could they do if such a situation was to arise and why.

**Encourage interaction** with siblings or arrange playdates to promote friendships and increased social communication.

Playing with other children is important. It develops their social skills, encourages sharing and helps them express feelings more freely **in a variety of contexts**.

**Reinforce turn taking**, it may take time for them to learn to listen rather than simply wait for their turn to speak.

Use 'structured' play together to demonstrate and let other children **demonstrate good social** and communication skills.

Try explaining and **demonstrating body language** and how to use it.

This might seem a bit ambitious but deciding to **have a discussion about a topic you disagree on**, ideally something impersonal like a story on the news, **can be very useful**. Learning to disagree calmly and constructively, accepting that just because somebody has an opposing view doesn't necessarily make them an opponent, is a valuable skill to develop. Learning how to **'debate, not argue'** can help them immensely in the future. In this age of social media people appear to be increasingly intolerant of differing views and tend to disregard or become hostile towards those who may have them, leading to endless upset. Your child will be happier if they learn to see things from another's point of view as well as be more constructive and know when to ignore unconstructive criticism.

## Social skills to consider:

Can you **see any 'gaps'** with your child in these particular areas? You can ask them if they think they are good at these and discuss:

- Asking for help
- Accepting differences
- Apologising
- Being patient
- Being responsible for their own behaviour
- Complimenting others
- Disagreeing 'nicely'
- Encouraging others
- Following instructions
- Listening attentively
- Resolving conflicts constructively
- Sharing things
- Staying on task
- Taking turns
- Participating fairly
- Showing interest in other people's lives

With any skill you choose together, **go over it, practise it, review it**. It is important to **discuss social skills with them**. A lot is expected of children but much of this can be too easily assumed.

After an incident, you can ask them to talk or write about what each person might have been thinking and feeling at the time and how they might be feeling afterwards (but first acknowledge your child's own feelings so they don't become defensive). This is a key skill to develop. It will not only **help their social skills** moving forward but also encourage them to be **less extreme** in 'writing somebody off' after a disagreement. It can also reduce their stubbornness and better enable them to understand how to repair relationships for instance after falling out with a friend.

Humans are naturally social creatures and if there is anything we've learned during the recent pandemic and related 'lockdowns' it's that children **need to be able to socialise** just as much as anything else.

**Ask them lots of questions**, especially using *'Socratic Questioning'* such as How..? and Why..? This improves their critical thinking skills as well as helps you to connect and shows you value their opinions and ideas, giving them a voice.

Also try to remember to **ask them about whatever they're doing**, watching, playing, etc.

Use open-ended 'higher order' questions so that your child is able to **respond at their own level**, and also can't just 'hide' behind closed yes / no answers.

**Higher Order Questions:**

What happened?

Can you give me an example of..?

What would happen if?

Do you have another idea?

Which questions could you ask?

How was this similar to..?

Can you explain how?

Can you tell me why?

What was the problem with..?

How could you change this?

*Can you think of any more higher order questions together?*

Encourage your child to **question what they see**.

For any quiz type activity, **discourage random guessing**. Giving their best educated guess is fine. But wild guessing means they're not taking a moment to try to process the information. This tends to stem from a lack of confidence rather than laziness. Every child loves to show how much they know (as indeed do adults, ever played 'Trivial Pursuit'? Egos are on the line!). Ask them to **think before they answer**. Remind them it's not a race (although some-times it might be) and give them a bit of extra context if they need it. Whenever they get an answer wrong obviously don't put them down. You can **use humour** or praise to cushion their 'failure' and remind them if they don't try then they'll never get one right any-way, but they at least need to think about it for a moment first.

# 9 - PRAISE

**Praise and rewards must be earned**.

You may initially need to **'praise normal'** to reinforce boundaries and expectations.

Praise the behaviour **you want to see** in your children.

Give praise and attention **whenever it is due**.

**Notice when** they are behaving well – try to **catch them being good!**

Recognise and praise **specific instances**.

Be sure to praise every effort and **successful achievement of new skills**.

Don't just praise achievements but also **character traits**, such as "You're so funny" or "You're such a kind child."

Praise should be constant, **proportionate and genuine**.

**Feedback should be regular** and reinforce things they are doing right, while also giving advice on ways to **improve in other areas** when necessary.

Rewards for good choices should **ideally be immediate**.

If using a behaviour chart, awarding the sticker or tick or star etc. **is the immediate reward**. The attached bonus they may receive that is associated with this can be deferred until the suitable moment.

Use praise to **model to their siblings**.

Make sure **praise is shared** among siblings if possible.

Sharing praise and the reason your child is receiving it also **boosts their self-esteem** and makes them more open to following instructions etc. in future.

# 10 - GIVING INSTRUCTIONS

Keep language **plain and simple.**

Keep your **voice calm and quiet**.

Sometimes it is good to speak slowly perhaps using **long pauses** for more effect.

If they find it difficult to follow a set of instructions already, do not ask them to do something **if they are busy trying** to follow the current instruction. If they are already struggling to do something you've asked them to do, try not to give further instructions while they are doing it unless you are confident they can handle it and not feel like they're being nagged.

**Don't give more than two-step instructions** if you think they won't be able to follow anything more complicated. Let them do things step by step.

Make sure they are only **listening whilst you are instructing**.

**Clearly sequence** the steps in order for them to follow an instruction or complete a task.

When issuing a command that they probably won't like, you can try the **'Say and spin' technique** – give them the instruction then instantly walk away before they can react.

You can give a **time limit** if necessary. Perhaps use humour in this, ask them how much time they think they'll need, do a countdown and make a funny noise when time is up.

Be **positive in your instructions** and expectations.

When giving an instruction, **speak clearly and concisely** when you have their attention.

Try to **avoid exaggeration**, kids tend to take things literally.

Give your child **time to process** and follow instructions etc. (for them to think, understand then respond).

If they haven't understood, **try re-phrasing** rather than simply repeating.

Ask them a **follow-up question** to check for understanding.

**Encourage questioning** for further clarification.

If a child is not doing what you want them to do, **tell them what you want them to do** instead. i.e. say 'Walk please' instead of 'Don't run'.

Sometimes it is useful to include **a choice in a command**.

Expect that sometimes the child will **not comprehend instructions or commands immediately**. If you are frustrated by this, try **not to let it show**.

Ask them to repeat your instructions or **explain what they think they need to do** in order to **clarify understanding**.

**Body language can help a lot**, i.e. when commanding your child to 'Come here' you can point directly down to the spot in front of you, adding impetus and urgency to your command. Or for instance when asking them to stop using the phone, imitate with your hand turning the phone face down on the table.

**Rephrase questions or commands** if they say they haven't understood it the first time.

**Avoid nagging**, you **should only have to tell them once** if they've understood. Constantly nagging them **dilutes your authority**. Try 'I've told you once already' or 'What did I just say?' rather than repeat the instruction itself. Let them know that once should always be enough and if it isn't, **then it is their choice** not to follow the instruction which will ultimately lead to a negative consequence.

# 11 - BONDING

**Ways to develop a stronger bond with your child:**

- Help your child feel safe by being calm and consistent.

- Be available and caring.

- Look for any deeper reasons behind their behaviour.

- Share fun activities.

- Keep in mind the challenges they face.

- Have realistic expectations (though always try to keep them reasonably high).

- Let them know you always have time for them.

- Help them feel like they are a good person even if they sometimes behave badly.

- Show your bond is strong even when things become difficult.

- Appear to stay strong and stable, even if you feel upset inside.

- Your bond helps them to recover after an incident. Interact with them to help repair it quickly after disciplining.

# 12 - BUILDING RAPPORT

Don't underestimate **the power of a hug**, so try not to be stingy when it comes to giving them out.

If your child is really starting to get to you and your relationship feels somewhat fractured (did you ever feel you dislike them? Don't feel too bad if you did, it's perfectly understandable at times), make them feel you love them **more than anything in the world** instead – challenging, but it works!

Negativity breeds negativity and vice versa. I once worked with a student who really drove me up the wall and we started to increasingly antagonise each other. However, somebody gave me an invaluable piece of advice and through gritted teeth I started to **let the child think I really liked them.** This very quickly and effectively broke down any walls between us and we eventually became genuinely fond of each other and still have a good rapport to this day. In this instance, this approach enabled the child to gradually let their guard down, feel more comfortable around me and realise they had my attention anyway (which he was desperate for after being emotionally neglected at home) so didn't need to exaggerate his behaviour with me anymore. The child was also then more upset when I punished / more pleased when I praised him.

You need to tell your child off for negative behaviour, but if they think you're telling them off just **because you don't like them**, they're more likely to **ignore the message**. If they think you like them, they'll know you're only telling them off **for a genuine reason** and will listen to the message more.

When a child is showing positive behaviour, try to **spend time**

**with them in that moment** to share the experience. They will start to **make that connection** and seek your approval rather than negative attention. Interact with your child at every opportunity **when they are making good choices** / on task.

Try to listen to their music, watch their movies, TV shows, etc., to get some **frame of reference** and also show you're interested, have more in common, etc. This helps **build rapport** and they may then be more willing to share some of your interests too.

**Show them more of your own life**. There's no need to live in separate worlds. Perhaps you could bring them to work for a little bit if possible? I had a newfound respect for my dad once I spent a couple of hours at his office. I could see how tough his job was and realised he was doing it for the family. He subsequently no longer needed to remind me how hard he was working for us!

If you are starting from a position where you feel you might have already lost the 'battle', remember a parent-child relationship is **rarely too fractured to ever recover**, it just takes more time and effort. Don't give up. Keep going with your strategies and share your experience with someone who you can 'soundboard' off. Remember, essentially your child **wants to be liked and loved by you**, even if they don't show it (in fact sometimes especially if they don't show it, hence them 'acting up' to hide it).

Listen to your child. Encourage them to **express and discuss** their emotions.

# 13 - EXPECTATIONS

Expectations need to be **set out very clearly**.

**Be realistic** when setting any tasks or targets to be achieved.

Establish **consistent expectations** and consequences, with a **focus on the positives**.

**Model expectations**. Show both good and bad examples (you can use their behaviour chart review – see Section 17 – at the end of the day to help reinforce this).

**Manage your expectations**. Be realistic and avoid feeling pressure – it can take over a year for real improvement in some cases.

Thinking about **how much behaviour change to reasonably expect** can help both you and the child stay positive and realistic.

The target behaviour **must be achievable**.

Focus on any 'areas for improvement' **one at a time**, step by step, to avoid them being overwhelmed.

**Expect them to make progress** over time. Keep expectations relatively high but without piling on pressure – this can be a tricky balance.

Expectations **can have a greater influence** than you might think. When teaching in London, another school in the borough made the mistake of inputting the results of an aptitude entrance test the wrong way round, so the kids who were supposed to be placed in the 'top set' ended up in the bottom one and vice versa. Both classes were performing more or less as expected of a 'top and bottom' set. However, once the error was discovered, a letter was sent home to their (understandably disgruntled) parents and the classes were switched around. **The consequence was** that the top set drastically improved in their academic performance whilst the new bottom set dropped off considerably. All after being told they were top or bottom then vice versa!

Is it your child's job to meet all your expectations for them regarding their life goals? Is it fair? Do they have **expectations of themselves**? Have you talked about this together?

# 14 - WHEN OUTSIDE TOGETHER

**Teach basic manners**. Model them. Encourage your child to practise 'using' them while giving them **extra responsibilities when you're out** together. For instance, having them pay at the checkout, ask the shop assistant if they have something in stock, as for directions, pay the bus driver, etc. is a good opportunity which also garners a **sense of responsibility** which in turn **boosts self-esteem**.

When out with their friends and your child misbehaves, try to discipline them in a way where you **don't embarrass them** but if they push you too far then you may have no option but to do so.

Often pulling them to one side and **having a quiet word** to remind them of the boundaries is more effective than a confrontation where they won't want to lose face in front of others, something that can lead to an unnecessary and unpleasant escalation.

Discipline quietly, preferably out of earshot or sight of their peers. However, if the problem persists, you might need to **make an example** of them. Don't let them think they can 'hide' from being punished while out in public. Then once you have them at home, you must make sure they **know for certain** that if they ever do that outside again then the consequences will be severe.

It can be a good idea before going out to agree a **secret signal** you can make to let them know they're in danger of crossing a boundary. This can actually be quite a cool thing to share together. For instance, say their name or clear your throat to get their attention then make the signal i.e. by pulling your ear or rubbing your nose. This can actually be a fun thing to agree upon, letting the child choose the gesture.

**Use 'the stare'.** The first time you use it, if they continue to misbehave you must come down on them hard, so that **the next time** you use the stare, they will know to get back in line immediately. If they know the boundaries then they should know when they're misbehaving, so you **shouldn't need to nag** them. 'The stare' can be more efficient and effective than repetitive commands.

**Talk to them before going out** to do something together, calmly reminding them of the expectations and the possible consequences if they behave well / misbehave.

Make sure they are not hungry before going out, especially if to a supermarket where they may crave and demand many things they see.

# 15 - HEALTHY HOME ROUTINE

It is **so important to have a healthy home routine**. It may seem a challenge sticking to it at first, but if you keep it simple and take things step by step, this will be a huge help to both you and your child in the long run. Otherwise you are inviting all manner of issues both now and further down the line. Don't expect your child to settle into a routine immediately. As an adult I still find it hard to keep a consistent bedtime and eating times!

Here's **an example for after school hours**, it's up to you where you put the times and activities:

- Home from school – snack.
- Wash.
- 30mins maximum screen time, or play with toys or do other constructive activities (Which ones does your child like to do? Can you think of any others?).
- Homework if they have any.
- Dinner with family.
- More homework? / 1hour max screen time (talk about what they're watching or playing) or ideally a more practical activity (especially together) instead (see Section 16).
- More constructive play / activities (encourage sibling interaction, playing with friends if nearby).
- Get ready for bed.
- Read together (always try to include reading in any home routine. 15-30mins is ok, the more the better – guided reading techniques are discussed in section 15.5).
- Lights out (we will cover sleep recommendations in Section 15.3).

Can you think of **anything else to add?**

Just make sure there's at least a little bit of truly **free time** in there. Some kids are **overloaded** – their parents think they are doing the right thing by cramming their schedule with all sorts of activities. However, all that extra effort can end up having the opposite effect if the child becomes unmotivated and worn out. Everybody needs some **downtime**, especially children who are still learning to be themselves.

Try to let your child know about any events coming up that day or week if they are easily **unsettled by change or surprises**. Having a big surprise can sound fun but some children don't like it as they have no control over the situation or can be unsure how to react when something unexpected happens – though of course this can be **an issue that needs to be addressed** so you can perhaps help them become more used to having little surprises first.

If your child **breaks the home routine**, does not do their homework or is disrespectful, you can **take away their choice** of what to do after dinner and replace it with something like household chores (please try not to use extra study as a punishment as that can have a negative effect on their attitude towards academic work).

**Give and respect their space**.

Try to find practical **problems you can solve together**. For instance, fixing something that's broken, scheduling a busy day, shopping for and then preparing a large meal, etc.

Ideally let them **have a designated area** that is *their* space, where they can play, read, study, relax. Remember they rarely get a moment's peace at school or when with friends or family. Allow them some 'alone time' in a place they feel they belong and are safe. This will **help stabilise their mood** and give them **somewhere to retreat to** and calm down if they are upset.

Try to **allow your child to at least sometimes choose**:

•     what they can read or watch

•     what clothes they wear

•     what to play

•     where to go

•     when to do something

•     how to decorate their room

•     who to hang out with (this can be difficult, as peers with 'bad attitudes' can have a huge impact if your child is at all impressionable – which most kids are. Rather than telling them their friends are 'no good', try asking their opinion of them in certain situations – let them realise any areas for concern themselves if possible).

## - <u>15.2 - Diet</u>

Diet is as important as anything else and can impact on **their mood and ability to cope**.

**Make sure they have regular, healthy** meals: Every three hours if possible. **Avoid** refined sugar, caffeine (check for this in low calorie fizzy drinks), saturated / trans fats and processed / junk / fast food.

**Avoid eating late**.

Make sure they have breakfast, lunch and dinner **every day**.

**Ensure they have** fish and poultry for protein for recovery, vegetables for nutrients, fruit and complex carbs for energy. Unsaturated fats are also highly beneficial, along with daily doses of omega 3 and vitamin C. You can easily research more about healthy diets for kids online.

You can also find multivitamins for children to help **balance things out**.

They need to drink enough water to **stay hydrated** throughout the day too.

**Appropriate bedtimes**. What bedtimes do you set for your children? Have you researched this? How do they react when you ask them to go to bed or get up in the morning? Are the times consistent? How about the difference between siblings' bedtimes?

It is every parent's responsibility to make sure their child is **getting enough sleep**. As you hopefully already know, sleep is as important as anything for a child's physical development, attitude and learning. If your child does not have enough sleep it will almost certainly have a **negative impact on their behaviour**.

Lack of sleep is extremely damaging over the long term. Some families go to bed when the parents go to bed, I've known many little children regularly going to bed around midnight or later and their minds are more like rocks than sponges the next day in school. **It affects their mood, growth, memory and concentration**. As a long-term insomniac I am only too aware of the issues a constant lack of sleep can lead to.

One challenge can be a **reluctance to go to bed on time**. To help combat this and help with preparation, avoid screen time just before bed and encourage reading at that time instead.

**Routine is absolutely key** here, for instance: Wash face, clean teeth, go to toilet, climb into bed, reading time, lights out.

Another issue to watch for is as the oldest child grows up, they tend to stay up later, but it's far easier to send all the kids to bed at the same time so the younger ones **end up going to bed later** too.

If your child doesn't want to go to bed, before issuing a warning remind them what they have lined up the next day. They may **initially be resistant** to going to sleep because they don't want to miss out on something or have their day to come to an end. Reassure them that tomorrow will be filled with more things to do that they won't be able to enjoy or do well **if tired**. You can also include **tomorrow's activities in a visual planner** on their wall.

**Not having enough sleep can affect your child's:**

- Health (it will affect their growth and immune system).
- Cognition (they'll find it harder to process ideas).
- Creativity (they will be less aware, creative and playful when tired).
- Mindset (they will be more likely to be upset or become temperamental).
- Behaviour and attitude (less energy and more negative).
- Focus (harder to concentrate).
- Memory (they won't retain as much information).

**Recommended hours of sleep** according to age:

| Age Group | | Recommended Hours of Sleep |
|---|---|---|
| Newborn | 0-3 months | 14-17 |
| Infant | 4-12 months | 12-16 |
| Toddler | 1-2 | 11-14 |
| Preschool | 3-5 | 10-13 |
| Junior School | 6-12 | 9-12 |
| Secondary School | 13-18 | 8-10 |
| Adult | 19+ | 7-9 |

Please **follow these guidelines** as best you can. Make sure your child has a **steady, healthy home routine** and that bedtime is set **at the same time and adhered to** every night (this is often a target on behaviour charts).

## - 15.4 - Screen Time

How much time does your child spend on devices now? What is their mood like afterwards? How do they react when you ask them to put them down? Are they using them just before bed? There are **many things to consider** in this relatively new issue parents are faced with.

**Limited screen time** is advisable. For devices such as iPads perhaps 30mins is a suitable daily maximum. Encourage more **constructive activities instead** (see Section 16).

Limiting your child's screen time can **really be a challenge** as constant use of devices can be addictive but having too much of it is becoming a serious issue, especially with the ever increasing popularity of game consoles, phones, iPads, etc. **It can affect a child's** ability to concentrate along with their social skills and general mood.

There are however some educational or cognitively stimulating games that **can be useful in moderation**, for instance 'Minecraft Education', puzzles or strategy games. If they are using an iPad or phone, try to have **at least a few such apps** on there to choose from. You can **look for new ones together** in the 'Google Play Store' or wherever else.

Kids have a **hyperactive risk reward system**. Be careful not to overstimulate it with social media, apps, etc. If overexposed to this, not then getting everything instantly or having everything to hand in real life can see them become moody or even depressed.

Try to avoid using devices **too often yourself** when you're with your child. Set an example and see what interesting things you can do together instead.

Make sure you **have a filter on the internet**. It is still mind-blowing to me how without a filter kids can find ANYTHING they want (or sometimes don't want) online. Morbid curiosity can lead children down a dark path and it can be hard to undo the damage of trawling online and for them to 'un-see' what they have been exposed to.

Even YouTube can have disturbing violent content, just as Twitter can have extremely explicit and gratuitous sexual content. Be wary. There are however some excellent **entertaining and educational** channels to subscribe to on YouTube so perhaps you can tell them to limit their viewing to such specified content. You can also put a 'safe search' setting on their device search engine and monitor their browser history **as an added precaution**.

## - <u>15.5 - Reading</u>

Reading together can be a **bonding, calming** process.

Reading regularly has as **great an impact on learning** as anything else. This also often **translates into better behaviour**.

The **difference in behaviour** between children who read and those who play on an iPad or phone instead is often highly noticeable.

Here are some **questions you can ask** when reading together:

- What do you think the story is going to be about?
- What kind of story is it?
- What do you think will happen next?
- Which characters do you like / dislike? Why?
- Can you think of a different ending to the story?

**As follow-up activities,** they can try writing fan fiction, drawing a picture, make poetry based on the story, draw story maps or flow-charts to show how the events in the story are linked, etc.

They can also do a **book review which can include any of the following:**

- Type of story: (i.e. fiction / non-fiction, also genre; adventure, fantasy, horror, mystery, etc; it can be more than one).

- Look at the cover, what does it tell you?

- Read the blurb – does it tell you enough / too much about the story?

- What is the story about?

- Describe the setting (When is it? Where is it?).

- Describe your favourite character. Why do you like them?

- What was your favourite part? Why?

- How did you feel when you read the book?

- Which parts did you find difficult to follow?

- What 'mark out of ten' would you give the book? Why?

- Can you think of a different ending?

- Can you break the story down into opening, problem, events, resolution, ending (i.e. make a 'story mountain').

- Can you summarise the story?

- Were there any parts that were meaningful to you?

- Was there a moral / message in the story?

- Did the beginning hook you in? How?

- Do you know any similar stories? How are they alike?

- If you were this character, how would you feel? Would you do anything differently from them?

- Was there any new vocabulary or information that you learned?

- Which was the most important scene for you? Why?

- Can you draw a character or scene from the story?

It might seem like a lot of questions but kids often love **being asked their opinion** on things, though they might be shy at first as unfortunately, rather than being asked for an opinion they are constantly fed them by adults instead.

**Take turns reading pages**; kids love being read to and it gives more freedom for imagination while it's your turn to read. Listen for their use of **expression when reading aloud**, it's a good way to check their level of understanding.

Before reading and discussing a story or topic, **set the context**, make it relevant to their life or experience or at least elicit ideas and opinions to pique their interest. This is also useful **as it checks** what they may or may not already know before you begin.

Ask them to **explain the gist** of what they've read after each page or chapter.

Can they **re-tell** the key elements of the story they have read?

Try to establish extra time for **daily writing with them**, perhaps 10mins before dinner. **Incentivise** it and try not to make it a chore.

It can be very frustrating working with a reluctant writer, but try to build it around **their interests**, mix it up with **other activities** they like such as drawing, and **focus on rewards** whilst avoiding punishments in this area.

Support them in transferring their **ideas from planning into writing**. Ask them to put the plan down on paper then **verbally expand** on it before moving on to the writing. **Use mind-mapping** whenever appropriate.

Provide opportunities for your child to **read or listen to stories** connected to the writing topic first.

Encourage them to **discuss their ideas** about the writing.

You can try **alternative methods of recording** their stories. For instance, drawings, storyboards, comic strips, writing frames (good for showing children how to structure different types of writing – ones that give sentence starters are especially useful in the early stages), etc.

Give them a **writing checklist** to go over their work with afterwards if they want to edit it a bit. This would depend on age and level. For example, for Grade 5 level they could check to see if they: 'Show what kind of people my characters are by what they say and do or how they feel.' It can also include grammar points. They should have such a checklist at school (ask their English or homeroom teacher) or you could help them make their own one for home.

Go over the **next steps** they need to improve their writing.

**Try fluency activities**. A good example is '1 minute, 3 minute', where you give them a sentence opener only, for example 'I picked up the magic wand and I...' They then have one minute to plan what they are going to write (jotting down a few keywords), and three minutes to write it all down. They don't have to complete the story in that time. See how much they can write in the three minutes and count the words together at the end. Then if they like they can finish the story after without any time limit (they invariably like to do this, especially if they liked the sentence opener).

Another fluency activity is **'drawing for writing'** where they can draw a picture then write about it.

Write a story including ten **random words** you have chosen together.

**Try accuracy activities**. For instance, grammar activities such as 'Everyday Edits' (you can search these online) where there is a paragraph with ten mistakes, see how many your child can find and try to correct.

**Avoid use of erasers** in writing. Explain that once something's been crossed out, it is NOT a mistake. In fact, praise and reward your child for attempting new language (and therefore making more mistakes – which they can then just cross out neatly anyway if necessary).

You can even turn video games, TV, movies, etc. **into writing activities**, i.e. reviews, think up stories for their prequels / sequels, and so on (see Section 15.6.2).

Watch the start of a movie or a selected video clip and ask them to write something about **what they think happens next** or even the rest of the story if they're motivated to do it.

Ask them to **stop and read back what they've written** every ten minutes or every paragraph. Does it make sense to them? Any obvious errors to fix? What do they need to write next?

**Spellings:** It might sound a bit old fashioned but the method of 'Look, say, cover, write, check' can still be very effective.

## 15.6.1 - Writing Diary

It can be productive to encourage your child to **keep their own writing diary**.

They can choose one from a stationary shop and decorate the cover and back **to further personalise it**.

**This 'diary' is for them**. It is theirs to keep and can be kept private if they so wish (some even come with a little lock on it). It is for them to practise their writing (please avoid the temptation to correct anything they've written in there) and to keep a record of and reflect upon things in their life.

**In their 'writing diary', they can for instance write:**

- About anything that has happened in their life, big or small.
- Stories. This can be any kind of story, true or not.
- Write a short story based on a picture.
- About people they know, places they have been, things they have done.
- What they think about anything.
- About how they feel.
- About any hobbies or interests they have.
- Films, music, TV, books, etc.
- Any relationships in their life.
- Any new words they have learned (usually at the back).
- They can also draw illustrations to go with their writing.

## 15.6.2 - Writing around Movies & TV

*For reluctant readers and writers it might be an idea for them to write about a favourite movie or TV show of theirs rather than a book. Here are some suggestions:*

Describe a character in detail.

Write a short story about one of characters in a 'subplot' (a separate story from the movie).

Write a short story about something different happening in the same setting (i.e. in the 'Star Wars' galaxy, 'Middle Earth' or 'Hogwarts').

Create a new setting for the original characters to be in.

Write in a different genre i.e. a science fiction adventure short story inspired by the movie.

Write a poem about the movie.

Make a quiz about the movie.

Research and write about how the movie was made or one of your favourite actors.

Write a prequel / sequel to the story.

Place yourself in the shoes of one of the characters.

Write about the story from the viewpoint of different characters.

Think of a different ending for the story.

Write a movie / TV review.

Compare it to others you have seen.

Drawing also helps:

Draw different characters from the story and add captions.

Draw different settings related to the story and describe them.

Draw a new character for the movie setting and describe them.

Draw a scene from the story and describe it.

## - <u>15.7 - Homework / Studying at Home</u>

**Planning, organising and time management** are key life skills that they can develop early through the process of doing their homework well and on time. This is one of the main reasons for being given homework, even if you don't agree with the setting of homework itself.

Your child might even WANT to study of their own accord given the right **motivation and conditions**.

Ask them to **explain** what they need to do / what the homework is about.

Give them a set amount of **time** to do it in (decide together).

Ideally **promote quality over quantity**.

Try to present studying as a positive learning activity, **not a punishment.**

Ideally have a little desk or at least **workspace** somewhere for them in the home. Try to make it a **distraction free** area.

Children should have a **dictionary and thesaurus** in their room, as well as a book to write **new words** in.

Encourage them to **ask questions, make predictions**.

Pay **attention to the child's demeanour**. If they look tired, perhaps allow them to take a short break if appropriate. It can be productive to provide regular **brain-breaks**, ideally something sensory / motor related (physical movement, NOT close-up screen time).

If they think the homework is difficult you can agree with them. You don't necessarily need to apply more pressure. Then walk away and come back maybe ten minutes in to **check they're on the right track** and then before the end to see how they're doing and ask how they've been getting on. Be sure to **praise** anything decent they've produced.

Be careful **not to let them become too dependent** on your support. Your role should be as a facilitator rather than a teacher. It is a good thing if they feel free to ask for help when they need it, but they still need to try to work things out for themselves first and give it a go alone (unless they really don't know what they're supposed to be doing).

**Fade support** as your child becomes more independent and is better able to accomplish the required skills to complete their work.

Using a **'challenge-o-meter'** can help take the pressure off. It also encourages self-reflection. Basically, it is a picture of a big thermometer signifying the scale of expected difficulty, with for example 'easy peasy' at the bottom and 'rock hard' at the top. You could put levels like 'not bad' and 'a bit tricky' on the way up from cold (blue / easy) to hot (red / difficult). They can then place their avatar on whatever they feel about the upcoming task. Reflect on this afterwards to see if their initial feeling was overly negative or confident and briefly discuss it together.

**Check in** on them doing their homework but **let them think** it's to see if they need a bit of assistance rather than because you don't trust them.

Ask them to **show you** when they've finished.

Once they've finished, allow some free time to **relax and play after** (i.e. not straight to bed).

If you give them any extra work to do, **link it to their interests**.

Schedule a weekly time to **clean and organize the work space**.

- **Try going through these 5 key points before they begin:**

o    When to start.

o    How much to do.

o    How to do it.

o    What finished looks like.

o    What to do next.

# 16 - ACTIVITIES TO DO AT HOME

'Playing' can **aid their development** in many ways.

*Each of these activities can depend upon **age / preference** etc:*

Lego, Meccano, construction toys.

Model making.

TOYS – ideally something STEM (Science, Technology, Engineering, Maths) related, which many fun toys can be.

Painting, drawing, colouring.

Hula hoop.

Hide and seek.

Treasure hunt.

'Telephone'.

'Playdo', puppets, marbles (fine motor skills).

Reading, picture books, pop-up books.

Ball games (gross motor skills).

Diary writing.

'Drawing for Writing'.

Cooking (supervised).

Computer / video games TOGETHER.

Going to the park / local play area.

Swimming.

Music, dance.

*Board games.

Puzzles.

Quizzes (they can also make their own).

Card games.

Problem-solving activities.

Gardening (or at least taking care of a few plants around the house).

Helping take care of pets.

**Day trips – let them take part in planning the itinerary and deciding what to take.

TALKING: about school, friendships, interests, etc.

Read children's news together online (i.e. 'First News' or 'Newsround') and discuss events from around the world as well as locally.

Handicrafts (fine motor skills).

Outdoor activities (gross motor skills – anything from sports to simply walking the dog, cycling, Frisbee, etc.).

Allow for exploration of a new environment.

*Board games are great (and are coming back in popularity) as activities which involve real communication with an **authentic purpose** (try a few popular ones first. Pictionary is very fun, while Monopoly can lead to war in our household!). Kids also need to **experience losing well** and winning humbly. Losing is a **key part of the growth process** and can help build resilience and a determination to do better next time. Children tend to learn less about themselves or the world by being allowed to win (which can also further nurture a sense of entitlement).

**Outside of the home there are many things to do and places to go. Check out your local 'What's On' guide. Often museums and galleries are free. Liverpool for example has a fantastic selection of museums, galleries, parks with play areas, etc. to visit that are all free and child-friendly, along with many paid experiences that are made for children. Are there any nearby forests, beaches or other areas of nature you can visit together? Nature is a great way to reduce anxiety and relax.

Let them **choose and lead** the activities wherever possible.

**Increase their exposure** to various interests and activities. Let them try different things out without any pressure. Also, just because they might not want to try a musical instrument or particular sport now doesn't mean they won't be willing to give it a go later on.

Is your child more introvert or extrovert or a mix of both depending on the context? Introverts tend to need to feel safe before opening up. Extroverts tend to need opportunities to unwind. It can be important to talk things out with either 'types'. If you have children that fall into both camps, **doing interactive activities together** can help an introvert come out of their shell while helping the extrovert focus and share.

Playing together **enhances relationships** and is a time you can *both* relax in a safe setting. **Games / activities you can do together** include:

Hotter colder.

'Simon says'.

Hide and seek.

I spy.

Make up stories (take turns saying what happens next. I recommend choosing the genre, setting and main characters first. This can be very fun).

Make a quiz.

Try doing a 'still life' drawing.

Pictionary.

Charades.

Card games.

True or false.

Guess the voice (need a few people for this one).

Do a drawing from their verbal description of a picture and see how accurate you are. Take turns with this.

Write words or draw pictures on each other's backs.

'Would you rather' (i.e. Would you rather be rich or popular? Would you rather lick a trash can or a toilet floor? – gross example but kids tend to like gross, within reason!).

Balderdash (give three definitions of an obscure word and try to guess which one is real).

# 17 - BEHAVIOR CHART STRATEGIES

Behaviour charts can be **very effective** at almost any age.

If **used the right way**, I have known them to be so effective that they transformed classrooms and even effectively saved a few parent-child relationships.

Remember, **be insistent and consistent**.

If you have two or more children, **give all of your kids** a chart if possible (they don't have to be the same).

There should be a focus on **shared ownership** of the chart.

**Choose the targets for the chart together** (but lead them to the ones you want).

These targets should **be SMAR(T):** specific, measurable (i.e. not just something like 'be nice'), **achievable**, relevant and (not necessarily) time related.

There is **no need to make too many targets**. If they can achieve even just two or three, the positive effect of this tends to spill over into other aspects of their behaviour. The chart essentially helps them **become used to following instructions**. If 'I clean my teeth' is a rule they learn to follow, then once they can clean their teeth alone without needing to be reminded, they will then be more likely to follow other instructions that aren't on the chart more independently too.

**Encourage independence** / responsibility with the targets (which in turn helps increase self-esteem / competence).

Keep expectations **high but realistic**.

Home charts **can be very simple**, such as three boxes for every day: i.e. brush teeth, have a bath, read a story. The targets can obviously be more advanced for older children.

They can put a star, tick or sticker in each box every time they do something without any upset. If they complete a day there's a mini reward, complete a week a bigger reward. It also **helps you record their progress** to reflect on later.

Agree the associated rewards **together**. When choosing their reward, **give them a selection** to choose from and they can also suggest their own if possible.

**Theme the chart together**. What kind would your child like? Superheroes, football, a favourite book or movie, vehicles, etc.? Are all quite popular. Brainstorm it with your kids. Some I've used are 'Harry Potter', 'Star Wars', Liverpool FC, 'BTS' and so on.

Ideally keep it posted **up on their bedroom wall**.

**Review their chart with them** at the end of each day, week and even month preferably in a moment when you are both calm and getting along well.

Try to 'catch' them being good, look to give them the stars (or ticks or stickers or whatever they use to mark their progress) whenever possible. Once they achieve a few, they will be much more eager to keep it going. **Focus on the good in order to see more good!**

Use the chart to **spend time reinforcing the targets** with your child now so you don't spend even more time having to nag them about these areas later.

The chart can essentially **act as a set of 'Golden Rules'** if you so wish.

In addition, you can write down a set of fundamental house **'golden rules' and all sign it together**. Choose around 5. These can be quite broad – unlike the more specific and personalised chart targets, for instance:

We are nice.

We use our gentle voices.

We respect each other's things.

We listen to each other.

We help each other.

You might want to **add something more specific** if there is a recurring family issue, for instance 'We take turns choosing what to watch on TV'.

# 18 - 'COLOUR CLIMBING LADDER'

I based this positive behaviour management scheme on a 'traffic light' initiative I was asked to help roll out in inner-city London primary schools years ago. I found the format to be effective but felt it needed more positive colours for kids to aspire to and it then became far more effective. Indeed, after a few weeks of bedding (or rather battling) it in, it completely transformed a challenging Year 6 class into one of the best behaved groups in the school. The use of this system, when being insistent and consistent, **cannot be underestimated** in terms of its impact. Some **key benefits** of the colour climbing ladder (or 'CCL') are that it is:

Practical.

Clear and visual.

Interactive.

Consistent.

Flexible. They can move up and down the ladder throughout the day.

Efficient (no more nagging or repeating explanation of boundaries or needing 'final warnings').

Sanctioning your child may feel too extreme for many 'minor offences', is more difficult to follow through with and can stir long term resentment if the reason behind it isn't talked through calmly before the punishment commences, while doing small incremental punishments can become a chore and lose their impact.

So, moving up and down the colours on a 'CCL' is more **efficient, immediate and flexible** and appears **fairer** to kids too.

Basically, the 'CCL' is a picture of a ladder of **7 colours** (a bit like a vertical strip with a rainbow on it) which they move up and down **according to their behaviour** and effort each day. Personally I use (from most negative to most positive): black-red-yellow-green-blue-purple-white. Green is the **neutral colour** which they start their movable avatar on **every morning**. Whichever colour they finish the day on is the colour they officially achieve, along with the associated sanction or ideally reward that goes with it.

I think it is good to have **red-yellow-green** in there, as it is similar to traffic lights / disciplinary cards used in sports so should already be familiar to them.

Often moving down or up a colour can be **punishment or reward enough**. Ultimately many kids care more about the colour itself than the associated reward / sanction.

Rewarding and sanctioning a child in same day can **send mixed signals**. The 'CCL' helps **clarify** this as it's whatever colour they finish on that really counts.

Make sure **they are fully aware** of every time they move a colour (it is more effective if you ask THEM to move their avatar) and why and **elicit a response** on this from them.

Moving up and down the colour ladder step by step is good as it is **incremental** and they **can still recover** from negative moves.

Moving all the way down the ladder in one move for something serious like hitting **helps highlight** how unacceptable that particular behaviour is in comparison to other misbehaviours. Likewise, if they **do something outstanding** like make a big effort to be helpful or produce a great homework etc. then they can perhaps jump up two colours at a time.

If you use the 'CCL' with more than one child, you can then also give progress-based **group rewards**, for both daily and weekly totals, i.e. how many 'points' they've gained. I tend to use -5, -3, -1,

0, +1, +3, +5 across the colour spectrum. This way they may **work together** to achieve a reward. This helps prevent jealousy, adds positive peer pressure and encourages togetherness.

The child MUST be involved in the process and **take ownership of the ladder**. Agree on the rewards and sanctions and the focus of the ladder (i.e. following instructions, being polite, doing home-work, etc.). Make this process as positive as possible, do not have any argument while agreeing on these things as it will taint the whole idea. You can lead them towards what you want but try to let them think it came from them.

**Theme** the ladder together: They can decorate and personalise both it and their moveable avatars. You can put it up on their bed-room or the living room wall and also make a mini one to carry outside if you think that might be necessary.

The rewards and sanctions should be agreed upon and 'set in stone' until you decide together to **update them** in the future.

If can be used for **both behaviour and learning** (all aspects).

Something like stopping pocket money or grounding them leaves nowhere to go. This scheme offers a chance of near-term **redemption**. 'Yellow to blue' is a common trend among some children who need those constant boundary reminders before focussing.

Yellow is very effective as **a chance for self-correction** before they go too far and end up on the bottom colour which, if the day ends that way, can create more negative energy. Sometimes a warning is all it takes to **get them looking up the ladder** again rather than down it.

Having them looking up the ladder is key and you can nurture this according to how you approach using it. The 'CCL' should be viewed as a **positive behaviour management system**. Start off by trying to give more positive colours than negative (again, 'catch them being good'). This also helps **reinforce the initial targets** more effectively.

If a kid worries about moving down the ladder it **can prompt sub-**

**conscious negative behaviour**. It is always better if they are **striving to move up instead**.

The scheme provides a **FRESH START EVERY DAY** as they start on green each morning – no baggage!

You can **ask them in morning**, 'What can you do to move up the colours today?'

Remember, you need to be insistent and consistent with this. It will only be **as effective as you want it to be**.

**Be patient**. It can take a little while for the ladder to really come into effect.

**Find your 'rhythm'** with it (so it's not too easy / hard to move through the colours).

Always make them move their avatar **up or down the ladder themselves**. If they refuse, calmly remind them that this means they must **automatically move down again**. It is **their choice**. Hard at first but if you are firm they will usually only dare do this once. Don't back down and follow through with any consequences until they realise their protests will only be counterproductive for them.

If they reach purple or especially the top colour, you can involve their siblings and **share with everyone**, helping reinforce the positive behaviour.

In my experience with this, if a child says they don't care about the 'CCL', it **invariably means they certainly do**, but see it as a threat to their power or are not confident they will move up the colours. The best way to overcome this is to make sure they move up more often than down early on in the process, so it's ok to be rather generous at the start whilst being careful not to set a precedent. If they really didn't care, they'd probably just humour you instead (it really was a battle for first month when trialling the 'CCL' in London, but ultimately it helped turn the entire class around).

You can attach points to each colour, for example black -5, red -3, yellow -1, green 0, blue +1, purple +3, white +5, and total them up at the end of each week, covering some **'How did you get there'** discussion, especially if they finish on a positive total. You can then give a significant reward if they reach a high overall number (set this as an agreed target from the beginning). This process also helps to **REVIEW, REMIND and REINFORCE.**

If finishing the day on a negative colour, you can ask 'Why did you get yellow? **What do you think you can do** to move up the ladder tomorrow instead?'

One drawback of the 'CCL' is the sanction might sometimes have to happen the next day (as it's not good to end the day on a punishment just before bed), so use this as a REVIEW REMIND REINFORCE process too, with a focus on **how they are going to move up instead of down** this time (don't just say something like 'No TV for you because you were bad yesterday!').

Purple is great and red is bad. White and black should be rare extremes and **must be treated as such.**

**Depending on severity,** straight to red or black offences include swearing and hitting.

Otherwise, ALL colour moves should **ideally be incremental**, with just one step up or down at a time.

Whenever moving them down the ladder, it is important to immediately **remind them** they can move back up as soon as their behaviour or attitude improves.

Make sure the ladder is on display **as a constant reminder**.

Some parents **carry a mini ladder** in their pocket when outside together. Any movement can then be updated on the main ladder once back home.

Whatever colour they finish the day on **should ideally reflect** how hard they've worked / well they've behaved throughout (don't let them convince you they've been good just by being nice at the very end of the day – I fell for that one a few times when starting out).

# 19 – 'CLEAN SLATE'

Try to start every day with a **'clean slate'**.

When you see your child first thing in the morning, try to remember any positive instances from the day before and **leave any negative baggage behind** – as much for your own sake as theirs. It's too easy to think 'Urgh, here we go again' and you instinctively pick up on any negativity. Look for anything positive at all first thing in the morning, it can set the tone for the day.

It is important to **clear the air and move on** after an incident so there's less emotional baggage as it tends to bottle up and come out later in other ways. Wait until you are both calm enough to talk through a situation as openly as possible to try to resolve any lingering issues.

**Keep an open mind** and keep your cool if at all possible.

# 20 - BEING POSITIVE

Enquire and probe about any positive things that **have happened each day**.

Ask what things **they like about themselves**. Encourage them to **expand on their answers**.

Be mindful that most kids and indeed people **tend to focus on negatives more than positives**. It is how we have evolved. Humans used to need to remember negatives more, such as like don't eat toxic berries, walk across a strong river, go near a wild animal, etc., in order to survive. Now we have a myriad of social, work and family complexities to navigate that also have negative moments which are now stressing us out far more than they probably should.

For instance, when giving feedback on a child's work, 'two stars and a wish' is a popular method. However, if I said you have a really nice shirt and shoes but your hair looks awful, which would you remember the most? As long as **criticism is measured and constructive** (i.e. instead of telling them their breath smells bad today, you could ask 'Have you tried flossing or using the water pick? I'm sorry but maybe a piece of meat is stuck in there from yesterday, don't worry it happens to me sometimes too') then there's less need to sugar coat it. It can be nicer to **give any compliments separately** so a child may take them in more without being preoccupied by a negative.

**Nurture optimism** and teach them how to **reframe a situation**, i.e. if something they wanted to do is cancelled, what else can they do instead? Teach them to make the most out of any situation. While accepting it might not be their preferred choice they can also hopefully reduce the feeling that 'all is lost' whenever anything happens that they don't like.

**Teach them to accept 'no'** without an argument. Remind them it's not the end of the world and focus on any positives at all. Let them know that no **doesn't mean no to everything**.

**Beware any negative instincts** your child may have which can lead to them overreacting on occasion. Also keep in mind that like them, we too can often be guilty of **assuming the worst**.

Help **talk them through** these negative instincts. Talk about how they can be an **unnecessary trap** and **ultimately self-fulfilling** if they don't try to work them out.

Remind them **everyone has their own struggles** and challenging situations. In this age of social media children are bombarded with relentless images and updates of people trying to always look happy and successful and popular. Help your child to see how this is an **edited version of 'reality'** that often makes others more insecure about their own lives. As hard as this may sound, encourage them to focus on the positives **by being more positive** in their attitude whilst always putting any **negatives into perspective**. Keep life simple, what do they really NEED each day? Does any problem automatically affect the 'big picture'.

Constant exposure to social media, especially from a young age, also instils an even stronger **sense of entitlement**, where if a child is not happy all the time then something must be wrong. One antidote to this is taking them to **help people less fortunate**, for instance bringing old toys to an orphanage, delivering meals to the elderly, taking part in a charity initiative, coming to play with kids in a school for the physically or mentally challenged, etc. This is win-win, as first and foremost you'll be helping people who might need it, and secondly it will help bring your kids down to Earth and show them **how challenging life can be** for others. It would obviously be great if they became enthused by helping others and want to continue doing this out of choice.

# 21 - ROLE MODELS

Find examples of people they like or respect who have gone on to be successful to succeed, **as a source of inspiration**. For example, there's plenty of famous quotes from disciplined sports stars such as Michael Jordan or Steven Gerrard about how hard they had to work and practice and how often they failed in order to eventually succeed.

Ask them who they think is a **good or bad model** for these examples. They can be people from real life rather than TV etc.

**Be a role model yourself** by being the person you wish your children to be. Sounds cheesy but it has little impact telling a child how to behave when they see you doing the opposite yourself.

The **way we react teaches them** how to react, for instance being instantly grumpy whenever a challenge appears. Think of yourself and your own parents, are there any behavioural traits you think you might have 'inherited' from them? When with your children are you playing out any issues you had with your own parents?

# 22 - BOOSTING ESTEEM

**Focus on what they are good at / what they enjoy**. Celebrate them being good at something, instead of spending more time panicking when they struggle in another area.

*Boosting esteem: Discuss or write down with them their strengths and qualities:*

Things I am good at.

Three things I am grateful for.

Compliments I have received.

What I like about my appearance.

Challenges I have overcome.

I've helped others by…

Things that make me unique.

What I value most.

Times I've made others happy.

**Model resilience** yourself. Try to exhibit more stoicism or practicality and be less reactionary when a challenge arises (difficult I know). For example:

'I'm disappointed that I didn't get the job, but that's because it was important to me. It's nice to have good things happen, but they don't always end up the way you want them to be. I did my very best in the interview and I know I'll be okay. Obviously that one wasn't the job for me, but I know there is going to be one that is. I just have to keep trying and be patient.'

It might seem like an unusual way to talk to your child but they should **value your openness** and the way you are talking to them on a more mature level.

**Encourage mastery** of even just one topic, activity or area (to take pride from). They don't necessarily need to be the best at it, such as the star striker on a football team, but rather be good at it **by their own standards**. For example, 'You're a superstar when it comes to trying new things. That's a really valuable skill. I wish I was like that when I was your age, in fact I'm not even like that now - maybe I can learn from you!'

Another reason to focus on any area of potential strength (i.e. music, sports, art) is so your child may take confidence **from this into other areas**.

Let them know they are **loved unconditionally** (even on the days they test your patience).

Esteem / confidence is a major factor. Kids tend to **compensate for insecurities**. For instance, one Year 6 pupil I worked with was an illiterate bully. We focused on his football skills to **boost his esteem**, and he became nicer in class and started to concentrate more and was subsequently less reluctant to work on his reading and writing. We made sure he knew we were working **with him** in order to help him, rather than forcing him to do something he hated (his resentment of writing came from the fact he was completely lacking esteem in that area from an early age). The bullying gradually stopped and by the end of the year he was actually quite protective of some of his classmates.

EVERY kid has something positive you can praise to help boost esteem. If you can't find anything obvious, **keep looking!**

**Individuality** can allow your child to further develop their level of independence and help boost their self-esteem. **Let their sense of identity evolve** along their own path as best you can, whilst trying to help them 'keep on track' – a difficult balancing act at times.

If there is any particular 'talent' or hobby your child has, remember to **refer to it whenever relevant** (without going overboard). This could be anything at all, even just whatever their latest fleeting interest might be.

Many issues stem from low esteem. In fact, sometimes the cockier a child acts, the lower their esteem – **hence their overcompensation** / attempts to cover it up.

There appears to be a growing trend in the number of depressed children out there. Although in my view social media certainly contributes significantly to this, there is also the issue of teachers and parents being encouraged to constantly tell their children **how special and wonderful they are**. The problem with this is that when these children come up against challenges they A) give up too easily because they aren't used to facing failure and B) become extra disappointed because rather than try to overcome the challenge, they might be more likely to wonder 'If I'm special and wonderful how come I'm rubbish at this?'

True esteem comes from children **being able to do things for themselves**, not just being fed false praise all the time. After all, if everyone is special, doesn't that contradict the meaning of special? **Not everybody can be great at everything**, so the sooner your child realises this not only are they less disappointed by failure but they will also really appreciate their achievements and be more likely to work hard toward any goals.

I remember when a primary school I was working at had a visiting Olympic gold-medalist weightlifter giving a demonstration. Afterwards the head teacher proclaimed to ALL of the 300+ children watching "There's no reason why any of you can't become an Olympic champion too!" It was nice for the kids to hear but seemed such a ridiculous statement. There is **so much emphasis** on 'If you believe it, it will happen' etc. that unless everyone becomes an actor or athlete or inventor or explorer or billionaire etc. then there's going to be a lot of disappointed young adults out there, just as there is now according to mental health statistics. It is great to be ambitious, but is that helped by being given inflated opinions of themselves that can't live up to reality, or getting effort badges for finishing last or being applauded for almost anything at all? The general message is 'everyone should be happy all of the time, if you work hard for regular pay you are a mug' etc., which to me seems like it's **setting kids up for a fall**.

They need to learn to react to negativity **without overreacting** or losing perspective or giving up immediately just because something doesn't come easily to them or due to a lack of resilience. Children ideally need to learn to **help themselves through challenges**.

# 23 - GIVING RESPONSIBILITY

**Give them responsibility**, i.e. tidy up, feed themselves, organise what they need and get things for themselves – this boosts their self-esteem and capability.

Always **give them chances to be trusted** (i.e. extra responsibilities such as carrying things, paying at the checkout, looking after their younger sibling, taking care of the family pet, getting something for you, answering the phone, etc.).

**Give them routine responsibilities** around the house. Walking the dog, feeding the fish (pets are a great way for kids to take responsibilities on in a positive and interactive way), collect the dishes after dinner, washing or tidying up, cleaning their room every week, changing the bedding, washing the car, tidying the garage or garden or backyard, watering the plants every day, helping a neighbour with something, reading with a younger sibling or friend's child... Can you think of any others?

**Encourage independence** as much as possible. Let them do things for themselves. Make them feel their ideas, choices, knowledge and experience are valued.

Let them watch you cook or **share the cooking**. **Ask them** about the ingredients, where they think they come from and how they are made, which ones could go well together, etc. Write the **family shopping list together** (you might need to remind them of the effects of eating too much sugar and processed foods before making the list!).

# 24 - BUILDING RESILIENCE

*Activities for building emotional resilience:*

- creative play.
- board games; good for planning, working memory, mental flexibility and impulse control i.e. taking turns.
- games that involve memory.
- challenging activities that test both their ability and patience.
- strenuous exercise.
- team activities such as football or basketball.
- persevering with something they haven't tried before, which they might not be initially successful at but can learn to enjoy and get some sense of achievement from.
- giving them opportunities to think and act independently.
- providing opportunities for them to make their own decisions.

**Help your child develop resilience.** It's difficult trying to **find a balance** between letting them know they can always ask for help, and teaching them when they need to try to cope with things more independently. Regularly **talking things through with them**, especially about expectations and responsibilities, can help you both find that balance.

# 25 - NEURAL PATHWAYS

A child's brain and **the way they react to things emotionally** can perhaps be compared to a jungle with lots of paths. The more they go down these paths, the more connected and easier and quicker to travel along they become.

For example, if a child becomes angered by losing a game, and this happens more and more and goes unchecked without any intervention, then they will be **easier and quicker** to be angry as it becomes a well-worn pathway (or 'go to' emotion) in their mind. If they continue to focus on their anger, it will become more of an issue.

We have to try to block off such negative paths off or at least make them longer or place certain 'obstacles' in the way, while also trying to **create more positive path** shortcuts as diversions / alternatives. This involves some **Cognitive Behavioural Therapy** which is something I've found very useful over the years in helping children become less reactionary and more reflective on their behavioural instincts. It is definitely worth doing a bit of research about online.

The older we get, **the harder it is** to change the pathways and the more effort it takes to do so.

*How to make a new path / close an old one:*

Ask your child…

To identify the problem. Why is it a problem?

What are the options / What can they do about it?

What can they do next time?

To plan it (how are they going to do it?)

Review things – after it happens next time, how did it go? (you can use the 'after an incident' question list in Section 27).

This all seems complicated but it **can work for the simplest** of plans such as 'just walk away and count to ten'.

Think of some examples and maybe even role play them together, or at least talk through some of the possibilities. Also, remember to discuss 'What's the worst that can happen?' (see Section 25.1 for a SWOT analysis) – though remember in their world something that might appear trivial to you **can feel relatively monumental** to them.

Encourage them to **think before they act** so they may develop the ability to resist the urge to do something as an immediate response that can have a negative long-term impact. Explain how 'If I can't think before I act, I can at least think beforehand about how to act in case a situation arises.'

## - <u>**25.1 - SWOT Analysis**</u>

Help them to **face their fears** with your support. You could do a **SWOT analysis** (Strengths, Weaknesses, Opportunities and Threats):

- How can you respond to each possible outcome?
    - What are the potential strengths of taking a particular action?
    - What are the potential weaknesses of this?
    - What are the opportunities from taking this action?
    - What are the threats of taking the action?
- What's the worst that can happen?
- What would [someone who they see as capable] do?
- What has worked before?
- Say as many ideas as you can in two minutes, even the silly ones.
- How can we break this problem down into more manageable pieces?

# 26 - ANGER MANAGEMENT

**Calming your child** can be a challenge when they are angry. There are many reasons they can become angry and they can show this in a variety of different ways, just as adults do, by becoming aggressive or passive aggressive, sulking, directing it towards someone or something else, becoming self-destructive, crying, going 'on strike', threatening to run away, and so on.

As a child I was taught that being angry was bad. My parents' response to me being angry was usually to become angry with me, telling me off for it. However, this would often not only confuse me but also **make me even angrier**. I would then sulk and release my anger in different ways that could sometimes be more destructive after 'bottling it up.'

An important first step for parents it to let your child know that **being angry can be normal**. After all, it is often unavoidable. Many adults become angry too – but it is **how we respond to our anger** that shapes events and in some cases our lives.

You can help your child **recognise and name** their anger (ask them what physical and emotional sensations they typically experience), which should in turn help them start thinking about and taking control of their own behaviour.

When your child is able to identify their feelings and realise that at that moment they are angry, **it helps reduce** the chances they will overreact. When we become angry, our common sense is 'bypassed' and we often do things we regret soon after. If a child knows they are angry, they will know that at that moment they might be out of control and in danger of making a poor choice, and so may therefore become more hesitant to act.

Through **sitting down and talking** about your child's anger with them, you can help them **identify the 'trigger'** of their anger, and assist them in finding a way to either break the habit of responding to such a trigger aggressively, or at least help them consider **alternative choices** they can make as a response before doing something they will regret. For instance;

walk away

take a few deep breaths

count to ten

count breaths

go to a 'calm place'

repeat a calming mantra or phrase in their head

tell someone

give themselves a little pinch to remind them it's not the end of the world

scribble something down about it

go and read (sounds far-fetched but I've seen it work)

draw

splash water on their face

run around

yell into a cushion

go and do an escape activity (i.e. go outside to kick a ball against the wall)

squeeze their hand closed and open repeatedly as if holding a stress ball

blow on their hands (looks a bit weird but can be surprisingly calming)

play with a pet

push against the wall (discourage your child to hit objects – we want children to let go of their anger without hitting)

Read books or watch films together that feature an angry character. Talk with your child about what the character is feeling and experiencing, the consequences of their anger, and perhaps **come up with ideas** that would help them cope better.

Calming down by themselves or 'self-soothing' is a skill that children **must learn**.

By encouraging your child to find a solution that helps them control their anger or even avoid reacting to triggers in the first place, you are helping them **feel in control of their emotions** and more confident in their **ability to handle difficult emotions**. Anger is a natural feeling to have and like other emotions it needs to be **expressed appropriately**.

If they are yelling at you, you can say 'I want to listen to what you're saying but **can't hear while** you're shouting. Take a deep breath and then you can tell me all about it'.

With teenagers in particular, sometimes they essentially just **need someone to listen** to them rather than be judged or given advice (which they will probably rail against in their anger anyway).

Remind them (and yourself) while they are calm, that it is extremely **difficult to make rational decisions** whenever angry or afraid, yet they will **still be held accountable** for their actions even if they think they have a right to feel that way at the time.

Suggest they learn to '**think for a second**' (essentially meaning stop and actually think for a moment) before reacting to something that has 'triggered' them. This way they can slow down and in not reacting immediately **give themselves the chance** to make a more informed reaction once they have taken even just a moment to process what is happening.

## - **26.1 Children Hitting**

*A child might hit somebody to:*

• Attempt to momentarily escape their own emotional pain by inflicting it on another.

• Explore cause and effect ("What happens if I hit them?").

• Experience the physical and emotional sensation of fighting.

• Try to put themselves 'above' someone to compensate for insecurities.

• Imitate other children and adults.

• Feel strong and in control.

• Get attention.

• Act in self-defense.

• With younger ones, in the absence of developed language hitting can communicate needs and desires, such as hunger or fatigue, or can be a form of interaction to get a response from the victim.

• Communicate or express difficult feelings, such as frustration, anger, confusion, or fear.

*What can you do to prevent hitting?*

• After an incident, make them 'regretful' and wary of doing it again as there must be a consequence that will make them unhappy. You can use the behaviour ladder to go straight to the bottom colour and apply the sanction that goes with it. It is also important for them to acknowledge they have made somebody suffer. Wait until they have calmed down to discuss them apologising.

• A clearly structured healthy home routine can help take unpredictable challenging behaviour out of the equation.

• Offer activities and materials that allow your child to relax and release tension. Some children like yoga or deep breathing exercises. Sports and games can also help children release tension.

• Use positive guidance strategies to help your child develop self-control. For example, offer constant little reminders of what the boundaries and expectations are, but only whenever relevant so you're not nagging them.

• They need to be told in no uncertain terms that instigating violence is completely unacceptable. Not only will it make others sad and resentful, but all that negative energy will only make your child feel worse inside too. And there will also be serious consequences.

• Use a reminder system to help your child learn to express strong feelings with appropriate words and actions instead of physical aggression.

• Reinforce positive behaviour by acknowledging / praising your child's appropriate words and actions in place of hitting, i.e. 'You didn't like being tickled so you used your words to ask them to stop and now everything's fine.'

• Provide opportunities for your child to make choices and feel empowered (so they're less inclined to use hitting as an option).

*What strategies are not helpful?*

• Avoid labelling a child as violent. Negative labels can affect how you view your child and more damagingly how they view themselves.

• Avoid getting angry yourself.

• Avoid giving too much attention to the child after an incident. While this is usually negative attention, it can still reinforce the behaviour and cause the child to repeat it.

• Do not force the child who hit and the child who was hit to play together afterwards.

• Do not to physically punish the child (doing so can also

undermine your relationship).

# 27 - AFTER AN INCIDENT

Use an **'after an incident' approach** to review situations / incidents and suggest alternatives for the future.

Clearly **explain when and why** the child has chosen the 'wrong' interaction and go through it with them.

Ask them to reflect and ask **what they could have done instead /** can do next time for a happier outcome. You can then model it and ask them to demonstrate to show they have understood (i.e. If a young child has been playing too rough, stroke the top of their hand and say 'See, I have gentle hands' and then ask them to do the same to you). **Try not to** simply tell them off then forget about it.

*After an incident Activity:*

Invite your child to write and discuss their answers to the following questions after a behaviour-related incident:

What happened?

How did I feel?

What did I do?

What did I want to happen?

What did happen?

What could I have done differently?

Would that have been better? How?

What will I try to do if it happens again?

It can be **very powerful to hug after** resolving a disagreement. It helps soothe the child (as well as yourself) and re-establishes the parent-child bond.

You are human and have your faults just like your children do. If on occasion, for whatever reason, you realise you **may have been unintentionally unfair** or overreacted, you should probably explain and apologise (no need to grovel, just be honest), otherwise you will 'lose' them a little bit each time.

Put it into context, i.e. "I'm sorry I became upset, I'm tired and it felt like you were just having a go at me." They will respect and appreciate your honesty and you can then **expect the same from them**. It also shows you are more secure in your parenting as well as open in your communication. Your child should subsequently feel better for resolving having upset you without them having to apologise themselves as usual (though they may well do so, for their part, in return anyway).

# 28 - SELF-ORGANISATION SKILLS

Self-organisation **can be a real point of conflict**, i.e. arguing because your child is slow to get ready for school, forgets what they need to bring or do, misses a homework, etc.

Create **checklists and 'to do' lists**.

Ask them to **estimate how long** their various tasks will take.

**Break down any tasks** (can use 'short burst' instructions, clear and specific).

Use **visual reminders** and **time planners** such as diaries, visual timetables, daily reminders, watches and alarms.

One useful tip is **keeping a list** they can go through of what they may need to bring with them next to the front door, so they can check they have everything before they go to school or wherever (I still need this for going to work!).

You could also designate a space (preferably near the front door or in their room) **for things they need** to remember to take for the next day at school etc.

Establish a **clear routine** for them at home.

Highlight / ask them **what the priorities are** for any task involving time organisation.

**Set clear time boundaries and deadlines**. Perhaps you can use a 'warning countdown' if necessary – try to make this a fun thing between you, like a race against time and you're the timekeeper.

Especially put **time limits on things that have become too open and frustrating** (i.e. getting ready for school). You can also make this a behaviour chart target with an associated reward. If they just miss the limit you can say something like "Ooooh, poor you, so close but just didn't make it, better luck next time" rather than shouting "Time's up, unbelievable, you missed it again!"

Ask them to write down the start and finish times for some tasks or activities, so they can **learn to 'budget' time**. Taking too long or rushing things can often be a spark of confrontation.

Try to ensure that your home / their room **is relatively organised** to reduce unwanted distractions and unnecessary disruption.

Make it clear to them (preferably by asking them without talking down to them) **why they need to do something.**

Help your child **maintain a 'to do list'** that they keep handy. It can cover both short and long-term things.

They should also definitely **have a calendar** on display in their room.

# 29 - MAKING MISTAKES

Encourage them to **take (safe) risks**.

Make light of mistakes while **avoiding ridicule**.

**Don't rush to their rescue** every time.

Let them know **you trust their capacity to cope** and grow through facing challenges.

Both you and your child **shouldn't be too afraid to make mistakes**. Everyone does. **Behaviour won't always be perfect**.

Help your child to 'learn to **learn from' mistakes**, as opposed to just becoming frustrated or giving up. Rather than them immediately thinking 'I can't do anything right', guide them to respond in a less negative way such as 'I can do many things ok but am just struggling with this one at the moment.'

Talk with them about **how making mistakes is okay** and part of learning.

**Share some mistakes** you've learned from / that have helped you become better at something yourself. As my father always said, 'If you never take a risk you never get better'. There's plenty of evidence to suggest that the more you practise and fail the more you eventually succeed.

# 30 - SPOILING THEM

**Don't spoil them** – they need to appreciate what they have. Most spoiled kids are in a state of constant dissatisfaction.

Some kids are *never* **satisfied** with what they have, as they are **conditioned to want** things (you can blame many external influences for that, such as relentless advertising campaigns or fads among their friends).

**If they think they can get what they want,** they will adopt all manner of strategies to manipulate you into giving it to them.

After they have what they wanted, they will just then want something else, and always asking for and getting what they want **can leave them constantly dissatisfied**, as they **never learn to just accept and enjoy** what they already have instead.

I've worked with children who have bedrooms stuffed full of toys they never play with and throw tantrums at toyshops because they want the next thing they think they can't live without. **Learning to accept they can't always get what they want** will help safeguard them from antisocial behaviour and tendencies towards depression in the future.

Sometimes you can give them what they want but make them wait for it first, so the learn patience while it also gives them a chance to get over the initial 'craving'.

It might be any idea to let them **do special chores in exchange** for extra pocket money (special because regular chores need to be done to contribute to the household without financial gain – we don't want to be raising mercenaries). This way they can learn the value of money and therefore appreciate it more if you spend any on them. They will also gain some sense of satisfaction of having completed a job and being rewarded for it. This will also encourage them to budget their hard earned income.

It should be beneficial to **let them see how less fortunate** children live. You could do this by visiting an orphanage or special school with them when you donate their old toys or clothes to charity for instance.

Spoiling your child doesn't just mean giving them whatever they want. It also applies to **letting them do** whatever they want, which can be more destructive.

There's a quote I saw online that said "Five minutes in the naughty corner now can save five years in prison later. Punish your kids so society doesn't have to," featuring a small child crying in 'the naughty corner'. I thought that was very apt. One thing I've noticed with challenging children is that much of their behaviour stems not from being deprived but rather **from being spoiled**. Without boundaries and appropriate life lessons, some parents are unwittingly nurturing sociopathic tendencies in their children. The toll a difficult child can take on their class's learning can often be detrimental to all. Their parents may then blame the teachers or pretty much anyone and everyone else before they take a look at themselves or their kids. In my experience, such parents have lacked the guidance they need, and such families tend to be in a constant state of disruption and are generally unhappy.

I remember being jealous of a childhood friend who was very spoiled, often getting whatever he wanted and rarely having to face up to any consequences. We are still close but he now struggles to hold down a job or maintain relationships as he tends to blame others for anything wrong in his life. He seems to think he should be happy without having to work for it. This **lack of resilience has really cost him** in the long run. He usually gives up easily on anything challenging so misses the sense of reward and achievement in overcoming difficult situations.

**Don't seek your child's approval**, it should typically be the other way around. Avoid overspending just to make them happy. Essentially they want **your attention and affection**. I've worked with some very materially spoiled children who feel totally neglected emotionally and they can eventually resent their parents despite having been given whatever material things they wanted at the time.

If you take your child to a shop, give them a budget for one item only and **let them decide**. This teaches them not only to try to find the best deal for the amount they have, but also that in making their choice they are accepting not getting other things in the shop they also may want.

# 31 - LET THEM BE BORED

Kids need **to learn to entertain themselves**. You don't have to be their constant entertainer. Let them be bored so they may develop ways (perhaps with a few helpful suggestions for you) to amuse themselves on their own. Otherwise, they will constantly be bothering you or their siblings if they have them.

**Allow them to be bored** sometimes. This helps their imagination and creativity develop as they find things to do.

Being bored also leaves them to **become more independent** in taking control and finding different ways to entertain themselves. You can remind them, only boring people become bored as there should *always* be something to do.

Letting them be bored is underrated and can be a valuable process. It helps **build resourcefulness as well as attention span**.

Don't feel you constantly need to **spoon feed them entertainment** or give them the iPad or phone just to shut them up, this can be the worst thing you can do as when you don't have anything for them they can quickly become disruptive. Instead they can be a **part of the room**; involve them in conversations, help develop their social skills.

# 32 - PLANNED IGNORING

**Planned ignoring** can be for you as much as them. Don't give **undeserved attention**.

This can be **challenging at first**, but once you start realising the benefits it will remove a lot of the emotion around it for you.

Sometimes the ignored behaviour can get worse before it gets better, as they become more desperate **in their attempts to get a reaction** of any kind.

The idea is that they gradually realise their negative attention seeking **won't actually get them any attention**, but when they stop it, that's when they can **get the attention they crave**. For instance, you can leave them out of conversations or activities until they stop being disruptive. **Your child wants your attention.** Use this positively **to help modify their behaviour**.

Actively **ignore low level negative behaviour**. As soon as they start showing positive behaviour, **immediately praise them and give them attention**. They will realise which behaviour can get you **to engage with them**, which in turn encourages **positive attention seeking**.

# 33 - ATTENTION SEEKING

Teach **more appropriate ways** for your child to get your attention, without feeling the need to 'act up'.

Teach them **how to request things** without demanding or begging or threatening to throw a tantrum etc. Make it obvious that if they do that, there's **far less chance** of their request being granted.

You can **ignore when negative attention seeking** begins, then perhaps just give a stern look which they **should understand to be a warning**. They should know the boundaries and know how they can seek your attention in a more positive way instead, so **give them a moment to readjust** after the warning before punishing them. In fact, punishing them would also be giving them attention – even if not the sort they initially wanted.

Give **positive attention throughout the day** so they **don't resort** to acting up in order to try to get it.

# 34 - OTHER FACTORS

**Nature vs nurture**. Don't think a child is 'born bad' or 'born good'. There are many contributing factors from when they are very young all the way through to adulthood. They do however still need to take responsibility for their actions, whatever any mitigating circumstances there may be.

Consider **environmental and emotional factors** that might be affecting your child - hunger, fatigue, anxiety, or unfamiliar situations or distractions can all make it much more difficult for children to control their behaviour. They are not always just 'being naughty'.

Underlying emotions also **impact their mood** and therefore behaviour. Being stressed by someone or something else, feeling rejected or neglected, jealousy, insecurity, etc. can all contribute to their behavioural responses.

This can be rather complex, there are a myriad of potential issues to consider. For instance, **exaggerated emotional responses** can also be related to exam pressure, a misunderstanding with a friend, fear of being gossiped about, feeling ignored, thinking they're being blamed for something or blaming themselves too much for something, feeling unlucky or victimised, feeling ugly (perhaps they don't like their hair, think they are too thin or overweight, are uncomfortable about their breasts or genitalia as they go through puberty, etc.), feel doomed to failure, thinking something is an absolute disaster and their life is ruined, thinking nobody likes them, and so on.

Remember kids **have off days** just like we all do.

Beware the basic problem of tired + hungry = **'hangry'**, at least on occasion.

# 35 - PEERS

**Take your child's peer relationships into account** and keep an eye on them as a factor in their behaviour. This can be a significant factor that can feel somewhat beyond your control.

When asking about their day at school, enquire about **their social interactions**. Breaktime is in fact usually the most important part of the school day for many students.

Try to **put yourself in their shoes**. The social and academic pressures of school, the trials and tribulations of growing up and adapting to things around them in an unforgiving atmosphere, etc. can be a harsh learning curve for many kids and can lead to difficult behaviour at home as a way of compensating.

Many kids are getting through school life one day at a time. It's usually a good idea to find out the topics and activities **that are coming up at school and go through** the basics of these with them. This could be anything from learning about the solar system to practising T-ball in the backyard. Children naturally compare themselves to their classmates so if they are capable in and out of the classroom it should boost their esteem and give them more confidence amongst their peers.

Encourage them to **make their own decisions** based on what they think is a good choice rather than for example simply following others' decisions or what they think others expect or want them to do. Go through hypothetical situations or past examples together and discuss what would be the motivations and consequences for the various choices they might make.

Teenagers are all ultimately exposed to the likes of drinking, smoking and sexual behaviour at some stage and peer pressure is invariably a factor in this. Look to **broach the subject with them** before it becomes an issue. Be calm and treat them as a young adult. Ask them what's going on, how they feel about it, what they know about it. Rather than lecturing them, ask them their opinion about for instance binge drinking, drug abuse or sexual promiscuity and discuss the possibilities and related dangers / consequences with them. Share your experiences and any lessons you or people you know may have learned. Let them know that you are there for them and that you want to support rather than judge, but they will need to be aware of long term consequences and how their friends might not always have their best interests at heart.

Make sure your child is aware how it is pretty much impossible to be **liked by everyone all the time** (even if they were, someone would probably resent them for it!), and **how valuable it is** to have a few quality friends, or even just one as can tend to be the case at least with younger children.

If you have friends whose children you think would have **a good influence**, or if there are any classmates or other peers you know of that you like, subtly find ways of having them spend time with your child so they may become friends.

# 36 - TALKING TO THEIR TEACHERS

Don't be shy to **use your child's teachers as a resource** (although be mindful yours isn't the only child they need to support). They have training, experience and most likely the child's best interests at heart. Feel free to ask them for advice about how to get the best out of your child.

Kids spend most of their waking hours at school. Building an **amicable relationship** with their teachers can obviously be very helpful (a benefit that often works both ways).

**Make sure their teachers know** about any consistent good behaviour or specific challenging behaviour at home.

*Questions you may ask your child's teacher:*

Social issues at school are usually most important to your child and can have a significant impact on their attitude and progress. Be sure to ask the teacher how your child is mixing with peers on the playground / in the canteen / in class.

How are they concentrating during lessons?

Which subjects / activities do they engage in most / least?

If you feel your child's school is setting too much (or even not enough) homework, talk to them about it.

Have they noticed any changes in your child's attitude lately?

Do they have any advice for what you can do with your child at home to help with their behaviour / learning?

Share some of your child's interests with their teacher so they can know how to better motivate and involve them in class.

What else can you ask your child's teacher? How is your relationship with them at the moment? How can you make it more positive?

# 37 - SIBLINGS

Their siblings (if they have any) also **need to see the reinforcement** of expectations and boundaries, rather than their brother or sister getting away with something.

Having said that, the child in question watching you praise and reward someone else for being good **can be more inspiring** (and less disruptive) than simply punishing them instead.

**Sibling rivalry** can stem from one of your children feeling less loved than the other.

Appear to treat all your kids **the same**. If you tell one child they're naughty and treat them like they're always naughty, they'll be much **more likely to be naughty**, and vice versa with telling them they're good. It can be a **self-fulfilling prophecy**. Try giving them the opposite feeling of 'being naughty' instead and see what happens (persevere with this). **Let them all think they are good**, not bad. The same can apply to academic ability.

If a sibling is better behaved, make sure it is clear any rewards they receive are due to their good choices, **choices which your other child is also able to make**, rather than any sort of favouritism. Use the success of a sibling as a good example rather than a source of resentment or jealousy. For instance, you could **ask them** 'Why do you think your sister got that reward? Do you think you might be able to get it next time? I'd love to see you get it too' rather than 'You see? Why can't you be more like your sister?'

**Avoid comparing siblings** – they will sometimes be actively looking for you to choose a favourite. They will want your favour, and conversely feel sorry for themselves and resent you if you appear to favour another. Either way you can't win so appear as neutral as possible.

# 38 - MINDFULNESS

**Develop their emotional awareness** by helping them identify, describe and work out their feelings.

Practise **mindfulness:** Observe and identify emotions.

Do mindfulness **exercises** like focusing on breathing, doing meditation or yoga.

Help them become aware of emotions as things to be **recognised and observed** and then it may be easier for them to deal with / act on them or not.

You can perhaps try the 'Headspace' app or TV series together to **guide** you, or something similar.

Children who can recognise their own feelings are **better able to remain calm** and deal with a situation, for example by processing a situation before reacting to it and using their words rather than challenging behaviour.

It might be an idea to **keep a 'feelings chart'** on the wall, featuring various emotions and their matching emoticons perhaps. You can ask them to tack their avatar onto whichever feeling they are having in the morning then in the afternoon or evening. Make them aware they can be experiencing more than one feeling at the same time but should choose which they feel most strongly at the time.

# 39 - EMOTIONS

**Encourage your child to talk about their feelings**: Help them to connect with them more, this empowers them to express themselves: 'Connect. Empower. Express.'

It is important for children to learn to **distinguish between different emotions.**

Remind them **emotions are temporary** and with practise they can learn to 'ride them out' rather than focus on them indefinitely.

**Acknowledge your child's emotions** even when you are not comfortable with them or think they are unreasonable. Recognise your child's viewpoint even though it may be different from your own.

When children **feel understood** it increases the likelihood that they will **share their feelings** with others in the future, thereby helping them develop more constructive **ways of dealing with their emotions**.

Encourage your child to practise **using words to express** their emotions.

Making your child feel understood and capable is also important for **developing their sense of self.**

Kids don't need to be and also **cannot be happy all of the time**. Let them know negative feelings such as anger, fear, jealousy etc are natural. It's how they recognise, express and deal with them that is the issue. Bottling up negative emotions rarely ends well as it tends to eventually come out in destructive ways.

Remind them that although some emotions aren't good at the

time, **they are natural** so shouldn't think there's something wrong with having them. It's more a case of **developing increased awareness and control**. They may simply be having a relatively normal reaction to an abnormal situation and perhaps just need to learn to self-regulate their emotions and subsequent reactions better. You can **share your own examples**, for instance recall and discuss a time you felt jealous, how you reacted and **what you learned** for the next time you experienced such an emotion.

**Try to avoid assumptions** about feelings and emotions. Ask them how they're feeling, and why, when you're in a comfortable and relaxed moment. Appear curious rather than nosey and try not to judge.

If a child is scared or intimidated, they may go into **'fight or flight'** mode. This is when their 'lizard brain' kicks in and as a result will be more reactionary and struggle to process information or the situation around them until they have managed to calm down.

Fighting, promiscuity, watching traumatising content online etc. can be **forms of self-harm** stemming from low esteem or past trauma. Help them **channel their emotions** into something else, ideally something more rewarding and purposeful such as sports, art or music. If they are starting to 'freak out', as an immediate alternative they can do something less harmful like snap an elastic band on their wrist or hold ice cubes to help temporarily distract from their emotional pain. Also consult the list of calming methods in Section 26.

# 40 - EMPATHY

Encourage your child to show empathy, firstly by being empathetic yourself. Model the behaviour you want to see in them. **If their siblings or friends are empathetic** this can also be hugely helpful.

Teach your child to **see things from another's point of view**. You can do this by asking about what they think characters in stories are feeling, what their motivations might be, are they completely good or bad. If the character is pure good or evil, is that realistic? Can they agree with a character's questionable way of thinking when considering the background of their particular point of view?

Some kids are easy to upset others but at the same time can be very sensitive to anybody upsetting them. This can often be due to only being able to see things **from their own perspective** and can lead to plenty of social conflict in the future.

# 41 - THINGS TO AVOID

**Avoid overload**. Despite best intentions, applying too much pressure and loading up a child's free time with 'forced' learning or extra-curricular activities can backfire as they have no time to be themselves or 'decompress'. Let them spend more time playing, let them be children, let them be themselves.

**Avoid hitting and shouting** – it is negative and leaves nowhere to go / teaches them to react aggressively (use words to find solutions that don't hurt anyone).

**Beware of transitioning without warning**. i.e. stopping them in the middle of something they are enjoying to do something they don't want to do, like from watching TV to going to bed (as for video games, it is unadvisable to be playing them less than an hour before bedtime). One solution is you can build up to it, i.e. give them a ten-minute warning, then remind them with 5 then 1 minute to go. Ask them to turn off the TV or stop whatever they are doing **by themselves** rather than you doing it for them.

If there is bullying among or by your children, try to remember **'don't bully the bully'** in response.

When you feel yourself becoming angry, take a deep breath, **take a step back** for a moment. Try to always be honest and understanding.

Be forgiving – once the child has been punished, try to **let go of any resentment** you may be holding on to, as it may well affect your attitude and lead to further unnecessary confrontation.

Being angry increases negative energy which they may feed off / mirror. Remain calm, hide your anger. **Express your disappoint-**

**ment in their choice**, rather than your anger with them personally.

## - __41.1 - Hitting Children__

While most people nowadays basically disagree with parents hitting their children, in times of stress, anger or frustration you **may well find yourself tempted** to do so. After all, parenting can be challenging and exhausting and some children, if they sense weakness and are trying to get what they want, will push their parents **to the limit**. But most parents feel guilty after hitting and may simply not be aware of the many **more positive ways of handling difficult behaviour** (if you have taken a moment to skim through this book I hope you will have found at least a few practicable alternatives).

**As an aside**, my siblings and I were smacked as children but generally only as a last resort when our behaviour was 'over the line'. We were usually only smacked once on the leg (not too hard) as an instant punishment and that was enough, as it was the idea of being smacked and the negative energy around it that we found most upsetting – forcing us to curtail our behaviour and go back into our shell – rather than any physical pain it may have caused. However, this did ultimately make for a rather tense and reactionary household at times.

Personally, I am generally against the idea of hitting. It is easy to do in the heat of moment but is at best only a **temporary deterrent** that perhaps provides a quick fix but very often **leads to increased fear, anger or resentment.** It also sends the **very wrong signal** that hitting is an acceptable response to a situation. Hitting leaves pretty much **nowhere to go** beyond that so if it doesn't work, it can be harder to revert to more positive disciplinary methods afterwards. Also, the day may come when they are simply too big to hit.

If you follow and implement what is in this book, I hope there should be no need for hitting. Hitting can be viewed as 'lazy' parenting where you haven't given **the time or effort** required to implement **more effective and less damaging** behaviour management strategies.

Some children may well 'deserve a smack', however the result could well lead to even worse behaviour further down the line. **Sanctions are often more effective** anyway. The sting of a smack wears off quite quickly, while the feeling of losing or missing out on something stays with them – and if you follow the various strategies clearly then your child should be aware they are being sanctioned because **THEY made the wrong choice**, not you. With hitting, **YOU are choosing** to hit them, and in that moment the reason for the hitting **can be instantly forgotten,** as the hitting itself becomes the issue.

## - <u>41.2 - Shouting at them</u>

What you are saying **is more important than** the way you say it.

Sometimes a whispered warning **can be more effective** than a loud one.

Using a calm voice **models good behaviour** (we have to remind our kids not to shout too).

Not having to shout **shows you're in control**, which sends an important message.

Kids are often **already somewhat desensitised** to shouting because of the nature of school life and interaction between friends.

You can raise your voice but try to do it rarely. It will also then **be more impactful** when you do this.

Never just yell, it **shows they've got to you** and you've lost control and they subsequently won't listen to you as much nor the next time.

Shouting models a negative behaviour that **you're trying to help them reduce**.

If you are shouting, this is **stressful for you too**.

## 41.3 - Use Alternative Language

**Avoid negative motivation**. For example, rather than yelling 'Don't shout!' you could **use the positive opposite** by saying 'Please use your quiet voice' instead – suggesting how to behave as well as modelling the desired behaviour yourself at the same time.

It might sound a bit unrealistic when your nerves are being stretched but try it, you will be surprised how much more effective it can be.

*For instance:*

| | |
|---|---|
| It's not that difficult! | Do you need more time to do this? |
| You think you're always right! | Would you like to take a moment to think about things? |
| Stop being naughty! | I know this is difficult for you but… |
| Just go away. | Do you need a quieter place to be? |
| Calm down! | Do you need some space? |
| Why did you do that? | I see you've… |
| It's not such a big deal. | I can see you're frustrated. Can you tell me what's bothering you? |
| Stop being such a big baby! | This seems to be frustrating you. How about we…? |
| What's wrong this time? | Is there anything you need? |
| Oh why don't you..? | Would you like to..? |
| Stop yelling! | Let's use our soft voices. |
| Oh will you stop crying! | Try to take a few deep breaths and then you can tell |

| | me what's bothering you. |
|---|---|
| Don't be so selfish and share with your brother right now! | I see you have a lot of those and your brother doesn't have any. Wouldn't it be nice if you shared some with him? (then praise after sharing and reaffirm how it was more fun for everyone thanks to them). |
| Sort yourself out, will you? | Let's see if we can fix the problem together. |
| What's the matter now? | I can see you're upset. Can you tell me about it? (LISTEN to what they say and save your judgement even if you disagree with them. They may calm down after getting things off their chest whereas if you disagree it will probably escalate into an argument instead). |

Can you think of any other examples? It might be fun to see how many you and your child can come up with together.

# 42 - OTHER HINTS & TIPS

**Win the small battles now to avoid a big war later**. *Choose your battles wisely*, you don't need to fight them on everything (for the sake of your own sanity). However, don't consistently 'turn a blind eye' to an issue. If you win a few little battles now, it will save you from having to fight a larger and more stressful 'war' later on. If they learn to follow one instruction or get back in line once then they are more likely to self-correct and do this again with less input from you in the future.

Using your authority effectively in one situation is more effectual than struggling to do so every single time. Children have more stamina and **can wear you down** so pick and choose your battles if necessary. If you do let them 'have a win', make sure they know it's because you've listened to them and understood where they are coming from and will give them a chance in this particular instance, rather than letting them think they've simply 'beaten' you or 'got away with it'.

Respect goes both ways. Don't assume. If you are fair and consistent **they will learn to respect you more** in time, although they may not express clear gratitude for this until they are much older – probably when they have children of their own and realise what you were going through!

Keep a **behaviour journal** to try to find a behaviour pattern and help identify any possible reasons behind the behaviour.

Nobody gets it right all the time. Remind your child that **nobody's perfect**, not even you. There will also be good times too, **make the most of these**.

Be specific about the behaviour in question. **Do not generalise your child**. For example, rather than saying 'Stop being naughty!', actually point out **the particular challenging behaviour** they are exhibiting and suggest an **alternative positive choice** they can make instead.

Use the **'Stop, Think, Do'** approach.

Simply telling a child to 'be good' is often not enough. When they are being difficult, try to **redirect their attention** to something that interests or pleases them.

If appropriate it can be useful to give your child opportunities to **go through and discuss together** any behaviour strategies that you are using or thinking of using with them.

Allow opportunities for **gross and fine motor-skills** (large and small physical movement) development.

Encourage them to **confront irrational fears**. For instance, if they are afraid of sleeping in the dark, you can gradually dim the night-light, or draw the curtains in the daytime and see if they can stay in the darkened room. At night stay with them when it is dark while they are falling asleep, perhaps whilst stroking their head. Praise and reward the longer they can stay in the dark room until they realise there are no sudden new dangers just because the light has been switched off.

It can help by **giving them a choice in which activity** they want to do, as this empowers them and makes them feel like they have some control. This can help motivate them and even prevent them from being difficult in the first place.

Focus on **one behaviour at a time.**

**Make time for creativity** and play.

**Let them talk**.

Three **key areas** to focus on when learning with them are: CON-IFDENCE, CONCENTRATION, COMPREHENSION. These all tend to be interlinked.

Over time, provide opportunities for them to direct their own actions with a **decreasing level of supervision.**

If they start making excuses, you can listen to them, but never accept an excuse unless there's a genuine reason or exceptional circumstance. Otherwise, they may begin conjuring reasons and qualifying their actions in their mind as they're contemplating negative behaviour in the first place. However, be mindful to **make sure the rules are always realistic and reasonable**. Sometimes they **might need adjusting** as your child develops or their environment changes.

Rather than simply telling your child they're in trouble, **ask them why** they think they're in trouble. They should usually know the answer, so then they're already reflecting and it also saves you from nagging them. After they answer, all you really have to do is give a suitable reminder via a choice (i.e. "If you can't play nice then you won't be able to play together until you can").

Acknowledge **you know what they find difficult** and make it clear that together you can try to find ways to make things better for them.

**Use humour** whenever possible. This can also help take the heat out of a situation (after all it's easy to take a situation too much to heart when you're feeling stressed and stuck together), but obviously not at their expense. I've always used humour whenever appropriate when working with children. Sometimes the more difficult a situation is the more useful humour can be (though obviously it can be very subjective).

Setbacks are usually only temporary and specific to a given situation. **Remind your child of this**, don't let them immediately feel down about life just because one bad thing has happened that they might still be able to overcome anyway.

# 43 - BE PATIENT WITH YOURSELF

**Be patient with YOURSELF** – there is no PhD in or perfect way of parenting! Do you always feel you should be doing more as a parent? That's natural. Keep your expectations of yourself reasonable. Don't be defensive. It's a steep learning curve that never seems to end, but at least you'll never be bored! Many parents suffer from 'imposter syndrome' – like they secretly feel they're not quite up to the job – so can overcompensate for this by becoming too reactionary or extreme in their methods.

Parenting is a **marathon not a sprint**.

Try to notice any small improvements in your child and take heart from them. You should **be proud** of any good that you see.

When flight attendants explain how to use the emergency oxygen masks, they always say you must secure your own before your child's. This approach can also apply to parenting. You need to **take care of and love** yourself if you are to take care of and love your child more impactfully.

Remember **your own stress** will lead to frustration which creates more negativity around and between you and your child. Take some pressure off yourself. Make sure you are also living for yourself and not just your child. **Look after your own wellbeing** as well as theirs. This will also help you avoid **bringing your own stress** into your relationship with your child, which they might mistake for being their doing.

Are you getting enough sleep yourself? How about diet and physical activity? Are you **making enough time for yourself** or to be with friends or taking opportunities to make new ones? **You are still you**, becoming a parent doesn't change that but simply adds to it.

Whether you'd like to believe it or not, your parenting skills **aren't 'the be all and end all'** of your child's development. Their overall environment and culture, schooling, friends, various experiences and myriad other external factors can also have a huge influence – hence why siblings very rarely turn out to be completely similar to each other (same parents, different external factors). There is only so much you can do.

**Be patient with your partner or fellow caregiver** if you have one, because at the end of the day you are in this together and ultimately both want what's best for your child. You don't have to agree on everything but still do your best to **present a united front** (not against the kid but rather for the kid), while always trying to remember to keep your child involved in the process so there's not an atmosphere of constantly 'talking down' to them or 'us against them'.

**Remain calm.** They will know you are disappointed from your words and any subsequent consequences. If you shout or make an angry face at them, you are modelling a negative reaction for them and increasing the negative energy.

Always remember the behaviour strategies and **don't give up on them too quickly!** If you start to fluster or lose your consistency **the child might pick up on that** and become more difficult as a result – things can be a power struggle to begin with.

**Take time to reflect.** Try to be objective about your successes and 'failures' of the day. Think what you could do differently next time. Be open to new ideas and give anything you try your best shot or it will fail before it's started – children can quickly sense any lack of conviction in a behaviour strategy. Mostly, think about your successes and how you can build on / use more of what is working. View any perceived failures as a learning process.

Parenting is something very few people can do without great effort and it is very **easy to put pressure on yourself**. It is an 'open ended' job, do what you can but don't feel it's never enough (because it never will be anyway).

**It can take a long time** for positive behaviour strategies to 'bed in', depending on the child and the environment. Focus on taking things 'step by step' and keep your goals achievable.

# 44 - YOU ARE NOT ALONE

Don't be reluctant to **make use of any support**.

Don't take it **too much to heart** if you are still struggling with your child. **EVERYBODY struggles** with their kids at times, even if they try not to show it.

Please remember that children may have one or more of **a variety of issues** which cannot be easily overcome in the sometimes limited moments you have with them.

**Share with friends** and family. Don't take it personally and put increased pressure on yourself if you are having trouble controlling your child.

**You can talk with** teachers, fellow parents, coaches, counsellors, your own parents, as well as research websites and TV shows, books and magazine articles, etc. There are many places you can go for more advice.

# 45 - SELF-REFLECTION ACTIVITIES

These activities not only **help your child contemplate** who they are and where they are at, also help to inform and **further develop your awareness** of their feelings and thought processes.

_'About me' Activity:_

Ask your child to write or at least discuss their answers to the following questions. Perhaps you can do the exercise together. Tell them anything they say, write or draw will remain confidential between you:

I feel good, happy, excited, calm, when...

I feel bad, scared, nervous, angry when...

I find ... difficult

I like to ...

I like ...

I don't like to ...

I don't like ...

I wish I was better at...

I think I'm quite good at...

I feel stupid when...

I feel clever when…

… is my friend

Write a list (perhaps using a time limit) of: Happy memories / People I like / Things I like about myself / anything else positive…

*What other areas can you add for discussion and reflection?*

*Emotions Activity:*

Together, **draw everyday things** that make you feel happy / sad (you can share some examples first).

Ask them to **write down all the emotions** they can think of. Then, **draw pictures** of simple faces to match them. You can then **make it into a game** where you then have to match their words and pictures together. Or you can take turns making facial expressions while the other tries to guess which emotion they are portraying. You can then discuss **which sort of situations** make them feel these various emotions. **Which ones** do they experience the most?

Write all the **things you like about each other.** They can also do this exercise between siblings.

Ask what sort of things upset them – then identify which ways **they may respond** in related situations.

Ask them to write down **one good thing that happens each day**. Tell them this can be anything 'big or small'. It can also be nice to keep a record they can look back on later.

_Feelings, friends and family questions:_

What makes you feel safe?

What makes you feel good?

What makes you feel afraid? Lonely? Embarrassed?

What makes other people feel like that? What can you do to help them feel better?

What makes your family / friends special to you?

What help do they give you?

What do you do for them?

What do you think they think of you?

How can you be good to yourself?

How can you show that you value other people?

How can you learn from the good or bad things that have happened to you?

When do you feel good? Confident? Grumpy? Upset? Nervous?

Who do you like? Who do you love? Who do you care about? Who cares about you?

What can you do when you are feeling worried or angry?

What does it mean to be grown up?

Now that you are growing up, do you have any new worries? Who can you talk to about this?

How do you talk to your friends and family? How does that make them feel?

Does growing up mean you need to take more responsibility for yourself? Can you give any examples?

What does love feel like to you?

What does hate feel like to you?

<u>*Talking about Personal Health:*</u>

*They might be shy to answer these questions so it can be better for them to just write them down and show you only if they want to:*

What is happening to your body?

What changes do you think will happen?

What effect do exercise and sleep have on your body and mind?

Why is personal hygiene important?

How would you describe your lifestyle?

Do you make healthy choices?

What dangers are there to your health?

What do you do to help the community? Is there anything more can you do?

How do your peers' lifestyles differ from yours?

How can you tell if strangers are trustworthy or not?

*With older children, you could perhaps try **going through questions** similar to these to help you both understand where they are at:*

What makes you upset? Which potential 'triggers' do you need to be aware of?

What helps you feel calm?

What helps you to concentrate?

What are your strengths?

What do you find challenging?

# 46 – HYPOTHETICAL SITUATIONS

Consider the following hypothetical situations and discuss them with your partner, a friend, your own parents, etc. – basically any fellow caregiver you feel comfortable with – then answer the questions numbered below:

A)   A child is throwing a tantrum in the supermarket. He is laying on the floor screaming because he can't have the toy or treat he wants. His embarrassed parents are standing next to him wondering what to do. His younger sibling is sitting in the shopping cart looking upset.

B)   A father asks his daughter to turn off the TV and go clean her teeth before bed. She tries to ignore him. He asks her again, but she still refuses to acknowledge him.

C)   A child comes home from school upset and goes straight to their room, refusing to talk to anyone.

D)   A child gives a Christmas wish list to their parents with a number of impossibly expensive items on it.

E)   A parent and child have an argument that escalates into an angry shouting match, after which the child runs out of the house.

F)   Can you think of any similarly challenging situations to discuss?


1)   What is the problem?

2)   What is the possible reason behind the behaviour?

3) What might an effective solution be?

4) If that doesn't work, what else could you try?

5) What would you do afterwards to help prevent such a situation from reoccurring? Are there any long-term strategies you would implement?

6) What can both the parent and the child learn from the situation?

Can you think of any other similar situations, either hypothetical or real? Try answering the above questions about each example you come up with. Are there any other aspects to consider?

# 47 - BEHAVIOUR MANAGEMENT CHECKLIST

*Each of these points are referenced in various relevant sections throughout this book, which you should read through for more detail:*

Look for **reasons behind the behaviour.**

**Never negotiate**. If they argue with you, deal with the rudeness before resolving the issue at hand.

**Appear calm**. This models good behaviour and shows they aren't getting to you.

**Stay positive.**

**Don't act in anger.**

**Give them a choice.**

Their behaviour **is THEIR choice.**

Maintain clear and realistic **boundaries and expectations.**

Be **insistent and consistent.**

**Pre-empt** rather than react.

Be **firm but fair.**

Always **follow through with consequences.**

Agree a clear **positive behaviour strategy** together, for instance **a behaviour chart.**

Use **sanctions and rewards.**

Praise and rewards **must be earned.**

Be **proportionate and gradual** with your consequences.

Don't **delay consequences.**

Give them increased **responsibility.**

Boost their **esteem.**

Build their **resilience.**

Develop their **self-organisation skills.**

**Stop. Think. Do.**

Use **positive (alternative) language.**

**Remain objective** – be disappointed with their behaviour, not them. They are **letting themselves down**, not you.

**'Carrot' is better** than 'stick'.

**Feedback and reflect.**

Give them **a chance to 'recover' their behaviour.**

Be a **good listener.**

Use **Socratic questioning.**

**Ask for their** opinions, thoughts and feelings.

Encourage **social interaction.**

Limit **screen time.**

Make **sleep a priority.**

Maintain a **healthy diet.**

**Let them have input** in the reward / sanction process and related targets.

Try to **catch them being good.**

You should **only have to tell them once.**

Instructions should be **clear and concise.**

Share **fun activities.**

Be **available / present.**

Share **hobbies and interests.**

Let them **know you love them** even when they are in trouble.

Keep **expectations reasonably high.**

**Read together** every day.

Re-establish firm boundaries in advance **before going outside** together.

Follow a **healthy home routine**.

Give them a quiet place to organise and do their **homework / study**.

Encourage them to keep a **writing diary**.

Use a **'colour climbing ladder'**.

Have a set of family **Golden Rules**.

Start each day with a **'clean slate.'**

Criticism should be **measured and constructive**.

Focus on **positives.**

Be a **role model**.

Allow them to **be their own person**.

Help them recognise and **manage their emotions**.

Reflect and review **after an incident**.

Try **not to spoil** them.

Mistakes **are ok.**

Let them **be bored.**

Talk with **their teachers.**

Beware **peer pressure.**

Practise **mindfulness.**

Encourage and develop **empathy.**

Avoid **hitting.**

Avoid **shouting.**

Let them **talk**.

**Don't generalise** their behaviour.

Avoid **nagging.**

Be **patient**.

Remember you are **not alone**. Use **support.**

Use **humour**.

Encourage **physical activity**.

Show them ways to **manage their anger**.

**Ignore** negative attention seeking.

**Don't 'bully** the bully.'

Encourage **independence.**

Let them **choose**.

Do **self-reflection** together.

# 48 - A FINAL WORD

The way we discuss children in this book might at times seem to paint a negative picture, but this is because we are talking about how to manage their behaviour when they are being challenging, as well as helping **prevent such behaviour in the first place**.

Essentially, **children want to be loved and give love in return in a safe emotional environment**. Sometimes we need strategies like the ones outlined in this book which might be hard to implement at first but should gradually help facilitate such an environment.

**Review with your partner or fellow caregivers** what's working and what isn't, parenting is always a work in progress after all. Develop a strategy that suits and give it time to take effect, it will be worth it in the end. Try not to **second-guess yourself** too much or expect things **to work straight away**, especially if both you and your child are new to the process. You will gradually learn to trust your instincts as you get into the rhythm of things.

**Parenting is a great leveller**. The most admired people in world history will have struggled with parenting, while I have friends who live relatively ordinary lives but are deeply committed, hard-working parents (and they too have their difficult days). For me, they are the **real unsung heroes** in life, because being a good parent usually results in there being more good people in the world. On the other hand, from what I have seen, some parents who have lacked the guidance or motivation to raise their children responsibly have produced people who unfortunately tend to bring more misery to the world around them. So, your efforts are deeply appreciated (even if nobody ever actually thanks you for it!).

I do hope you found this book interesting and managed to pick up at least a few hints and tips to use on your parenting journey. Thank you for taking the time and effort to be **open to new ideas and try new strategies**. I would like to wish you the very best of luck going forward and remember, you **can only do your best** in what I expect are sometimes difficult circumstances.

Peter Allerton.

For **children's stories** with a slice of weird and a twist of funny, please visit my blog:

**www.peterallertonwriter.blogspot.com**

_**The Peter Allerton Children's Book Anthology** contains:_

_The 'Smell of Poo' Children's Book Collection:_

    The MisAdventures of Mr & Mrs Poo

    Stanley and the Poo Monster

    The Poo Princess

    The Secret Adventures of Fartboy

    Ghost Poo and the Haunted Toilet

    Plus 2 bonus 'Pooems': 'Your Poo & You' + 'Who Dunnit?'

_The 'Beastly Bullies' Children's Book Collection:_

    Doctor Gremlin and the Battle of the Brats

    The League of Disgusting Gentlemen

    Jack and the Wish Factory

    Peter and the Pet Catcher

For ages 6-13, available in both eBook (accessible on any device via the Kindle reader app) and paperback, these stories tend to slightly increase in reading level as they go along – all the way from the first to the ninth.

There should be something for everyone to enjoy in this Anthology, including younger and older kids as well as their caregivers and teachers alike.

Every story features a set of 'follow-up questions'. These unique and humorous tales might be a bit revolting at times, but they may make you think a little bit as well... Anyway, I do hope you enjoy reading them!

Thank you for reading my book. If you enjoyed it, won't you please take a moment to leave me a review at your favourite retailer?

'Ta very much'!

Printed in Great Britain
by Amazon